EDUARDO MONDLANE

PANAF GREAT LIVES

Eduardo Mondlane

Panaf

LONDON

SBN 901787 24 8

Published by
Panaf Books Limited
89 Fleet Street, London E.C.4Y 1DU
Printed in Great Britain by
Cox & Wyman Ltd., London, Fakenham and Reading

The author and publisher thank members of Frelimo for their encouragement and cooperation in the preparation of this book, and for providing access to Frelimo documents.

The author is particularly indebted to Janet Mondlane for making possible Chapter 18, *Eduardo the man*. This chapter was compiled from tape recordings made during talks with her in Dar es Salaam in 1971. Grateful thanks also to Janet for the photographs, and for making available for publication two previously unpublished documents, *The Development of Nationalism in Mozambique*, and *The Crystallization of a Struggle for Freedom* (Appendixes One and Two), both by Eduardo Mondlane. The *Message from the Women of Mozambique*, a talk given by Janet at the World Congress of Women held in Finland in June 1969, forms Appendix Three.

CONTENTS

PLATES

Introduction

OUT of the long and hard struggle in Mozambique, leaders of heroic and noble stature are bound to emerge, some of them with less faults and who would make fewer mistakes than Mondlane. Nevertheless, he will remain in the hearts of the people, oppressed, degraded and downtrodden for five centuries, as the leader who helped them to climb the initial and perhaps the most difficult steps in their protracted struggle for freedom.

Mondlane belongs to an era when awakening Africa began to produce its first generation of nationalists to head the anti-imperialist struggle. He was a product of the universities of Witwatersrand in South Africa; Lisbon; and Oberlin College and Northwestern Universities in the United States of America. Academic honours were heaped upon him. His could have been the soft and easy life of air-conditioned offices and halls, or the serene and airy life of a university campus. And few could have pointed a finger at him. But he had his own powerful conscience to reckon with; for how could he live such a life when his companions were groaning under the weight of increasing oppression, and the people crying out for a lead?

The intellectual, historically, is a product of the capitalist system. Its institutions have moulded him. His training is such that he fulfils an important function namely to disseminate the ideas of the dominant class whether through the schools, universities, the press or the pulpit. Intellectuals by and large do perform that function and thus enslave the minds of the people to the acceptance of the ideas, values and mores of the dominant economic group in society. But a few intellectuals break loose. They cut the umbilical cord that binds them with the ruling class and cast their lot with their people. These men are viewed with hatred by the ruling classes. That is understandable, for capitalism opens

9

the vistas of its world in the fields of science, technology, culture, economics and politics. It also provides the key to the understanding of the system with its various ramifications and intricacies. The intellectual who is given this knowledge is expected to buttress this system, because the system also gives him a privileged position. But an intellectual who understands this system, detaches himself from it and ranges himself with the historical forces engaged in its overthrow is regarded as a mortal enemy. Such a person is pursued for the rest of his life and if he refuses to be lured back to the fold by inducements, then he is destroyed.

Mondlane was an intellectual of high calibre, academically well qualified in sociology and anthropology. The rulers believed he would spend his life teaching about the various tribes in Africa and also be the author of some treatises on this subject. In short, the life mapped out for him would be that of an academic who would fossilize slowly in the rarefied atmosphere of the university campus. Mondlane however had other ideas. While studying he also absorbed those ideas that would bring about the emancipation of mankind from oppression and exploitation. When the time came, he put these ideas at the disposal of his people, so that they could become intruments for their emancipation.

The ruling classes never forgave him for this, particularly when after the founding of the real national movement in 1962, he embarked on armed struggle. Under his leadership, the guerrilla war steadily developed momentum and ideological clarity. By the time of the Second Congress of Frelimo in July 1968, large areas of Mozambique had been liberated from the Portuguese, who could nowhere feel safe from attack. Frelimo's political work among the masses and the experience of armed struggle had resulted in a growing ability to distinguish between the forces at work for, and against, the people's movement, although it was still essentially nationalist in character. Speaking at this Congress, Mondlane attacked the NATO powers and American imperialism, but praised the socialist countries for their support. In particular, he singled out the People's Republic of China and its leader Mao Tse Tung for praise. It was clear then to the rulers that he would never allow his movement to be infiltrated and subverted by elements hostile to the Mozambican Revolution to which he was totally committed. Like other revolutionaries, he too was marked down for liquidation. So it was that on the 3rd of February 1969, as Eduardo Mondlane was going through his normal daily routine, he collected a parcel supposedly containing a book sent from West Germany about an early Russian revolutionary. The parcel instead concealed a bomb which, on opening the parcel exploded in Mondlane's face, killing him instantly.

Reactionaries believe that by physically annihilating a revolutionary they destroy not only him but what he stood for, – that the ideas and movement die with the man. The opposite is usually the case. The ideas and the movement become stronger than ever. For in perpetrating these dastardly acts, the reactionaries create heroes and martyrs. Today Guevara lives through his ideas and heroic example, meaning much more to the youth of the world than when he was alive. So too with Mondlane. From a leader of the Mozambican Revolution, he has become one of the heroes of the African Revolution, along with Moumié, Lumumba, Pinto, Ben Barka, and others who have been killed by the agents of imperialism.

than in the abstract that he would ...... allow his involvement to be abstract and articulated by ...... closure to the Mexican Revolution to which, he was particularly attached (the ...... resemblance he ...... east must of ...... republican. So it was that even the grid of Latin ideology, a Eduardo Mendive was ...... though he ...... could early run since he tolerated a partial appreciation ...... at those with the ...... of the ...... a spread ...... a ...... (a mixture ...... those ...... Tropi ...... a ...... a battle which was open to opinion and gaged expelled to abandiane where killing him became ...

Remembering to have that the ...... simplicity, and during a metaphorically they blame not only ...... but what they used upon what the ...... and ...... with the team. The opposite is usually the case. The idea and ideology on event become inanimate than even for so demonstrating there she smile itself, the ...... report figure, and analysis. There have a two through an idea and hence remains meaning much there to the smaller the world man who she was since. So too with identifiers. From a leader of the Mexican Revolution ...... along with Manuel, Carranza, Plato, but the country of us also have imbibed by the nature of ...... etiquette.

I

Early life

Eduardo Chivambo Mondlane was born in 1920 in the Gaza District of southern Mozambique. He was a son of a chief. Chieftainship is an integral part of the tribal system, and in it the chief occupies an honourable position. Before the colonial period they were leaders of their people, but were responsible to them and owed no other loyalty but to them. Portuguese colonialism, first representing mercantilism and later capitalism undermined the tribal system, destroyed its equilibrium, but nevertheless incorporated some of its institutions into its own system. One of these was chieftainship. The result was the transformation of the function of the chief as the leader of his people to one where he was the instrument of the colonial masters. Where a chief resisted and refused, he was removed and a 'nobody' was appointed to take his place (this is the word the Chope people used to describe the stooges). Mondlane himself described this transformation of the institution of chieftainship from a people's instrument to that of the rulers. He said 'To facilitate the work of the administrators, and the chefes do posto, the Portuguese government re-established a limited traditional authority for several African chieftains ... All African chiefs were made directly responsible to either the circuit administrator or the chefe do posto. Even more important was the fact that the chief's power no longer derived from a concept of legitimacy within traditional society ... The chief was no longer the leader of his community, but the representative within his community of a hierarchical colonial authority.'[1]

In many cases the chiefs were as poor as the few thousands over whom they ruled. It was not surprising then that Mondlane though the son of a chief spent his early childhood as a goat herd. His brother like many Mozambican youth was drafted to work in the gold mines of the Witwatersrand where he died of pthisis – a lung disease afflicting those who work in the mines. Another brother lost his life while working in the Mozambican docks. Mondlane acquired his rudimentary education in a protestant mission school, but he was refused admission to a secondary school because by the time he had completed his primary education colonialist law ruled that he was too old to enter. From this as well as other such experiences, he learnt bitterly what it meant to belong to an oppressed people. At even an earlier age, oppression had invaded his very home when his two elder brothers had to run away from him in order to escape the hated corvée system where the colonial masters would descend on the people, round them up and force them to perform free labour.

Mondlane's advance blocked in Mozambique, he made his way to South Africa to further his education. Overcoming many odds, he was able to pass his matriculation examination at a secondary school in northern Transvaal and thus was in a position to knock at the doors of the university of Witwatersrand. This was in the forties, when Witwatersrand, to counter overseas criticism of closing its doors to the blacks, admitted a few. At its height the University of Witwatersrand did not have more than 300 black students in one single year out of a total white student population of 5,000. Mondlane then was one of the privileged few.

That he went to South Africa was not unusual although the official language here was English and Afrikaans, and not Portuguese. Ever since the discovery of the gold mines in the Transvaal in the eighties of the nineteenth century the economies of Mozambique and South Africa were linked together in one vital respect, labour. As early as the beginning of the twentieth century the Chamber of Mines of South Africa had contracted with the Portuguese government for the colony to supply a hundred thousand workers annually to work in the mines. They were to work for a pittance of £3.00 per month. It was on the basis of this cheap labour policy that the mine bosses made millions.

Because the economy of Mozambique was a stagnant one, with little prospects of remunerative employment many

Mozambicans went to South Africa on their own. Such entry was regarded as illegal by the authorities, but so short was South Africa of cheap labour that they turned a blind eye. Thus many sought employment in the farms as well as in secondary industry. South Africa was then, as it is now, the most industrialized area in southern Africa and therefore acted like a magnet to the surrounding areas. If they did not come in as recruited workers through providing labour for the mines, they made their way by simply crossing the boundary. This is what workers did from Bechuanaland (Botswana), Swaziland, Basutoland (Lesotho), Southern and Northern Rhodesia (Zambia), Nyasaland (Malawi), South West Africa (Namibia). Even workers as far as Tanganyika (Tanzania) went to work in the mines.

Mondlane entered South Africa therefore at a time when a whole generation of workers had come and gone to the mines from Mozambique. He however entered when there was an awakening of the people of South Africa. The Second World War had left its mark on the oppressed people there. The most conscious sections of the intellectuals had begun to throw off their blinkers and cast off the mental chains which had restricted them for so long. This stirring assumed a political form when they took the bold and decisive step to demand equality with the whites in all spheres of life from the political to the educational and residential. The most conscious section from the oppressed had not only rejected inferiority which had been instilled into them, but also the more insidious ideas and policies clothed under sweet sounding phrases like 'Developing along your own lines' and words like 'Trusteeship'. As early as 1943, this stirring was expressed by organizations of the Africa people, like the All African Convention to which the African National Congress once belonged. The Ten Point Programme embodied the minimum demands for the coming period. This document was indeed historic, for the first point was the franchise whose realization meant the death of the policy of white supremacy. In a similar spirit of equality, it demanded a transfer of land to the tillers, who should own it, and thus end land hunger which is the driving force of the South

15

African revolution. Likewise its policy of non-collaboration with the oppressor was aimed at cutting the links between the oppressor and the oppressed. This meant the boycott of dummy institutions like the Bunga in the Transkei, the Native Representative Council (N.R.C.) and the Advisory Boards, which were institutions designed for a child race and evolved so that the people do not demand the genuine franchise which would give them levers of real power. It is small wonder that these ideas caught the imagination of intellectuals amongst the oppressed found now in the universities and secondary schools.

It would be expected that this new breeze would blow into the universities. The only university in South Africa open to the blacks at that time was Fort Hare, where courses were limited to the training of teachers and priests, and where there were no facilities for lawyers, doctors, engineers, dentists or architects. But now, in addition, the universities of Cape Town and Witwatersrand opened their doors. This was only for a short time, however, as the Nationalists on coming to power closed them once again.

Mondlane entered Witwatersrand University thirsting for knowledge. There he was introduced to the world of sociology, psychology, economics, political science, philosophy, logic and so on. There were books in their thousands waiting to be read, absorbed and digested. He could compare the poverty of literature in the African mission schools to the richness he found at Witwatersrand. In the lecture rooms he was bombarded with concepts like 'nation', 'class', 'tribe', and 'status'. He had to learn the theories of Hobbes, Locke, John Stuart Mill and other 'intellectual giants' in their own fields. He had to find his way through the labyrinth of the devious reasoning of Hegel, Kant and Whitehead. But outside the lecture rooms, he heard earnest discussions in the local cafeteria of men like Karl Marx, Engels and Lenin. He did not find many of their books in the university, nor were they discussed seriously in the lecture rooms. But he met those who called themselves communists, for the Communist Party of South Africa was not yet banned. There were many clubs and societies at the university. There was freedom for

16

anyone to say and write what he liked. It was the end of the Second World War and there was the belief amongst the liberals that South Africa would never be the same again and therefore fresh thinking about the country's 'racial problem' needed to be aired. Mondlane became acquainted with religious bodies like the Students Christian Association (S.C.A.) and the Students Zionist Association. There was universal sympathy for the Jews and their trials and suffering at the hands of the Nazis. Their plight was similar to that of the oppressed Africans and therefore the most radical of the white students, some of whom genuinely cut across the colour barrier, were Jews. However, what attracted Mondlane as it did the conscious section of the African students were political associations like the Diogenes Club, the Progressive Forum and the Students Liberal Association. There were also other associations which gave themselves no names, but which met as regularly as once a week and hammered out ideas not only about the nature of oppression, but the techniques adopted by the rulers to maintain oppression and exploitation. There was broad agreement, but controversies began on how to bring about the change in society. Many liberal lecturers had argued very seriously that the oppressed should work for economic emancipation and educational upliftment before asking for political rights. Such thinking was found also in the student study groups. The moderate groups preferred to style themselves as realists and practical men.

Decisive battles that bring about a radical change in society are never fought out in universities. The outcome of revolutions have been decided in the past on the barricades and now recently in the hills, forests and plains. Therefore too much must not be made of the role that a university can play. But the universities can and do act as sensitive barometers of coming storms. They, before other layers of society, catch with their sensitive antennae new ideas that are blowing into society. If these ideas belong to the oppressed and exploited, if these defend the aspirations and interests of the downtrodden, then the ideological battles take a serious turn. They cease to be mere verbal and semantic exercises. Such new ideas did permeate the university of Witwatersrand when Mondlane was a student and at times when such ideas fought it out for the mind of the student there would be bitterness The fiercest battles however were those when ideas calling for the violent overthrow of the old order were pitted against those calling for the maintenance of the status quo.

The universities are the training grounds for the future leaders of the system in capitalist societies. The university of Witwatersrand too was playing its role in grooming future M.Ps., M.P.Cs., Municipal Councillors, Secretaries to ministers, editors of newspapers and company directors. In short, the articulate radical student of today was being groomed to be the real pillar of society of tomorrow. And it was with these future rulers of white society that Mondlane discussed, argued and debated at cafeterias, tutorials and on the lawns. Here also he was able to clarify his own ideas. The open supporters of white supremacy were few in number and they were not vocal at all. Mondlane's chief ideological opponent was the gradualist, who said that he opposed the oppression by the whites, but was totally opposed to the oppressed people resorting to the 'extreme' method of armed struggle because it would cause a great deal of suffering and bloodshed. It was the gradualist's belief that the cause of the oppressed was served far more effectively if its leaders went about the task constitutionally and made the rulers understand the gravity and seriousness of the plight of the oppressed people. Thus the gradualist favoured round table conferences, petitions, or meeting this or that minister and presenting a memorandum. He was even opposed to boycotts which he thought were 'negative'.

At Witwatersrand, Mondlane was subject to the full blast of liberalism. There was no escaping it, for the friendliest lecturers who lent a willing and sympathetic ear to his personal problems were liberals. The most vocal of the students who at public meetings spoke out against injustices against the blacks, particularly black students, were liberals. One target of attack in those days was the pass law. And the police, both white and black made a particular point of harassing and humiliating students to show who was Baas (master). The Witwatersrand university was not in any way special, for he encountered liberalism at the other universities he attended, but his experience here stood him good stead. Liberalism as expounded by Hofemeyer, Hoernle, Ballinger in the forties stood for maintenance of the status quo in society, but insisted on reforms here and there to stave off a violent revolution. The liberals being relatively far-sighted believed that with the economic wealth in the hands of the rulers who were moving towards a modern industrial society, it was possible to share part of it with the blacks. Particularly, they believed that the educated and the propertied amongst the blacks should be granted concessions to prevent them casting their lot with the propertyless proletariat.

Liberalism ran counter to the call for 'equality' which had become the cry of the rising generation of black intellectuals. There was no racialism in this cry for it was equality of all and for all, including the whites, irrespective of race, colour and creed. But acceptance of liberalism meant acceptance of white tutelage which, however softened by smooth words, meant the hated status quo. Therefore the new generation fought tooth and nail with all the logic and argument at their command.

For Mondlane the time spent at Witwatersrand was also fruitful in another way. The decisions and debates went on till late at night and helped to clarify and crystallize his ideas. Increased political consciousness manifests itself at a certain stage in the creation of organizations. In the case of Mondlane it had already resulted in the formation of the Nucleo dos Estudantes de Mozambique (Nucleus of Mozambique students). The leaders of the group were students in the secondary schools. Because of this, he was thrown out of South Africa by the Malan government.

Organizations, whether they be trade unions, cooperatives, sport bodies or student associations in an oppressive society cannot but have a political orientation. The student organization of which Mondlane was the founder member could not confine itself to organizing student dances and socials when they saw clearly the acceleration of the mounting tempo of oppression. In the case of Mozambique they saw a whole nation's future was being stunted because the Portuguese refused to accept the basic duty of giving elementary education to its inhabitants. Nucleo thus became political. It was then that the 'government ... pounced on its leaders, put them in prison and proceeded to try to purge it of all political connotations ... having been one of the founders of Nucleo, I was also put in prison and thoroughly investigated by the state police (PIDE)'.[2]

Mondlane thus from his own personal experience had seen the identity of interests between the governments of South Africa and of Portugal under Salazar. The racialists of Lisbon were seeing eye to eye with the apostles of apartheid as early as 1949. It was the Malan government of the Nationalist party which handed him over to the Portuguese state authority although he himself had committed no crime against the South African government. It is acts like these that made Mondlane think of the struggle in the southern Africa context, rather than one for Mozambique alone.

2

Rise of the Mozambique National Movement

THE national movement as a phase in the struggle against imperialism is a modern phenomenon. At the end of the nineteenth century, a group of the most industrialized states in Europe conquered and annexed the remaining part of the world not already under their control. This flowed inexorably from the law of capitalist development where the individual capitalist, the much vaunted entrepreneur was sent to his grave and on which now stood the monopolist and financier. The result was the export of capital instead of commodities. Since returns on capital require a longer time than ordinary trade, the investors had to acquire political control as well. The export of capital was thus connected with annexations and conquest. The result was two-fold. The continents of Asia and Africa were colonized and its people once free were now a nationally oppressed group. On the other hand this conquest blew sky high the tribal and feudal economies and replaced them with capitalist modes of production. This was the general pattern. It differed here and there as in the case of Portuguese conquests. However the essential features were the same.

One such feature was the dispossession of the peasantry from the land. Whether it was in South Africa, or Kenya or Mozambique; whether they were British, French, Portuguese or Belgian colonialists they all had this in common. What happened to the peasants in Europe in the 15th to the 18th century, where they too were rendered landless by the operation of the processes of law, took place in Africa as a result of conquest. But the essential difference between Europe and Africa is that in the case of the former, the landless peasantry became transformed into the modern working class. No such thing happened in the colonies, precisely because the colonial powers never wanted industrial development to take place in its colonies. The operations of the capitalist system meant that they had become part of the money economy. They had no land, being dispossessed. But neither could they find work in the towns due to the underdevelopment of the country. Thus they were shunted to and fro with neither roots in the land nor the towns. This harassed, hounded section with nowhere to go, with nothing to lose, formed the backbone of many a national movement. The demand of the dispossessed peasant, suffering from land hunger made the agrarian the key question and the cardinal factor in most of the national movements of Asia and Africa.

The specific feature of the Mozambique situation was that the African peasantry was dispossessed not only to make way for the settler plantation owners and large companies, but like the South African peasants, was smoked out from their subsistence life by the iniquitous system of onerous taxation. This meant that they had to have ready cash, which meant working for a wage. Here a large section was recruited to go and work in the gold and coal mines of South Africa. At a time when the most advanced industries in western Europe and America were employing about 100,000 workers, the mines in South Africa were employing by 1910 more than 400,000, a quarter of which came from Mozambique. There the people who were nationally oppressed were also the most exploited. At the base then, the oppressed and exploited were one and the same people. Mondlane was able to see the genesis of his national movement flowing from, and as a reaction to, colonial domination. He saw its identity with the other national movements. For he said: 'Mozambican nationalism, like practically all African nationalism, was born out of direct European colonialism.'[3] The source of national unity is the common suffering during the last fifty years spent under effective Portuguese rule. In Mozambique, it was colonial domination, founded on the experience of discrimination, exploitation, forced labour and other such aspects of colonial rule which created the basis for psychological coherence.

The Africans like the Asians did not willingly allow themselves to be conquered by foreigners. They resisted and fought. Mondlane writes: 'Even as late as the second decade of this century, in 1917 and 1918 to be exact . . . the Mokombe (king) of the Barwe, in an attempt to re-establish some of the power of his legendary predecessor King Monomotapa staged a successful revolt.'[4] It was not a national revolt; it was confined to one or two tribal kingdoms. It was only when it was crushed that active resistance ceased.

Such defeats which resulted in the supplanting of the tribal and feudal chiefs and monarchs by the capitalist states were not due to any inherent superiority of the white man over the black man. It was not only the question of arms, although that is how many of the blacks who fought saw it, but that the capitalist system was able to mobilize the resources of the entire nation, economic, ideological, military, political, and launch it against a tribe or a princely state. Thus while they sought to divide tribe against tribe, pitting one tribal leader against another, they themselves presented a united front. Thus Mondlane with his knowledge of other national movements as well as tribal resistance had come to the conclusion that any form of struggle based on ideas other than the unity of the people was bound to fail. The Makombe of Barwa had showed that any resistance along tribal lines however heroic would not succeed. By the time Mondlane had left South Africa he had been convinced that the struggle had to be along the lines of a national liberation movement with political freedom as its primary objective. His years in Portugal and the U.S.A. far from changing this belief only served to reinforce it. However, it was only in 1962 that it was possible to form FRELIMO (Frente de Libertacao de Mozambique), the national movement of the Mozambican people which was to play an important part in the transformation of their lives, and which is also bound to change the course of Mozambican history.

Two factors, however, accelerated the formation of Frelimo. First, the fifties was a period when movements, national, regional and tribal in essence, but all calling themselves 'national' mushroomed all over Africa. And what was more, to the people at large it appeared that the rulers had decided to give in to their demands and to grant the freedom they requested. Of course few understood then that imperialism had decided to grant political independence in order to ensnare them further within the orbit of economic exploitation. The petty bourgeois amongst the Mozambicans and those politically conscious felt that something had to be done, and therefore believing that they should not miss the boat by default, began forming organizations. It might be said that when the people gave these their support, they believed that in this way they would be able to get their freedom. The first of these was UDENAMO, the Mozambique National Democratic Front (União Nacional Democrática de Moçambique), founded in 1960 in Salisbury, Southern Rhodesia. It was followed in 1961 by UNAMI, National Union of Independent Mozambique (União Africana de Moçambique Independente) based in Malawi; and MANU (Mozambique African National Union), formed in 1961, and consisting of those working in Tanganyika and Kenya. It was clear to Mondlane that these three political organizations based in three different areas, having support on a regional and tribal basis would never be

23

able to fight effectively the monstrous oppressive Portuguese colonial machine. Kwame Nkrumah, leader of the national movement in Ghana, was already propounding the idea of continental unity and was urging all the political movements of the same country to come together into a united Front. However, what was decisive in the case of Mozambique was the granting of independence to Tanganyika in 1961. Prior to this event Mwalimu Nyerere had met Mondlane and had indicated that he was free to use Tanganyika as a base to launch the struggle to liberate his country. President Nyerere with his experience of TANU (Tanganyika African National Union, founded in 1954), also showed by practical example the advantage of a single national organization spearheading the struggle. Mondlane referring to the role that President Nyerere personally played in urging the various organizations to come together writes, 'President Nyerere personally exerted influence on the movements established in the territory to unite.'[5] The result was that on 25 June 1962, the three movements which were then based in Dar es Salaam merged and the Mozambique Liberation Front (Frelimo) was formed. The unity of the three organizations paved the way for the holding of a national Conference which was held in September of that year.

Nkrumah and Nyerere who were admired by the Mozambican nationalists were outsiders nevertheless. What was needed was to have a Mozambican who would weld the three political groups into a single national movement. And in Mondlane the people of Mozambique found their man. Although at the time he was living abroad, he was in close touch with the people of Mozambique. He visited the country while on leave from the United Nations where he was working as a research officer in the Trusteeship section, and was able to gauge the mood of the people. He was also in touch with the three political groups, but for obvious reasons did not want to identify himself with any one of them. They all three asked Mondlane to join them individually, but he insisted that the only way he could join a political party for independence of Mozambique was if they would promise to take immediate steps to unite with other Mozambican groups to form a united front. After all these groups had promised that they would, Mondlane went to Dar es Salaam and helped to organize the Conference in which the Mozambique Liberation Front was formed.

During the crucial years of 1961 and 1962 he spent his time campaigning for unity of the liberation movement. As he stood above tribal and regional affinities, he became identified as the leader of a unified national movement. It was not surprising therefore, that when the first national Conference of Frelimo took place, he was elected its first President. He held this post till the day of his assassination.

3

The establishment of a National Front

THE present national boundaries of African states are mostly the arbitrary creation of the former colonialist powers. It is surprising how so many governments have accepted them, and enforced them with such zeal and efficiency as to make a mockery of the Pan African ideal. The people however do not recognize these divisions, and cannot understand why the concept of an 'alien' should apply to anyone born and living in Africa. Just as there are about 100,000 Mozambicans working in South Africa, and thus being responsible for the wealth that is South Africa's, so too there are, according to Mondlane, about 100,000 Mozambicans in Tanzania. Kenya had a community of about 200,000 working in the various dockyards. Others worked in Rhodesia and Malawi. Rrepresentatives from these as well as from Mozambique itself came to the founding Conference of Frelimo in September 1962.

This year, 1962, could be regarded as a turning point in the history of the people of Mozambique, for it was then that they first established a national Front in Frelimo. The conference was held in Dar es Salaam. There were representatives of almost every region from Mozambique as well as every sector of the population. Taking part were those who had experienced years of underground political work in Mozambique and most of them had tasted the brutality and savagery of the Portuguese secret police (PIDE). At the Conference were 80 delegates and 500 observers. Mondlane was satisfied for he says: 'All in all, the first congress of our party, was a very representative affair, in spite of the fact that it was the first of its kind in the history of our country.'[6]

The significance of the first Congress of Frelimo lies in its definition of the aim of the Front. In the words of the preamble, the Congress of Frelimo: 'Having examined the present needs of the struggle against Portuguese colonialism in Mozambique, declares its firm determination to promote the efficient organization of the struggle of the Mozambican people for national liberation . . . and to employ directly every effort to promote the rapid access of Mozambique to independence.'[7]

The principal aim then was national liberation which meant the end of Portuguese colonial domination. It rejected other aims which amounted to anything less than that. The Conference considered 'that the recent reforms promulgated by Portugal were within the framework of the same colonialist spirit that has typified Portuguese action for centuries; that because they were taken unilaterally, even if they were fair to the people, they would still be unacceptable.'[8] It was thus that the call of the first Frelimo Conference was for the rejection of these bogus reforms and a call for a fight for independence.

What was to be the basis of this unity? Was it to be the unity of the black man against the white, or was there another basis? Mondlane was quite clear when he said: 'The Mozambican national unity was born out of common experience in suffering together while working as forced labour on the large sisal plantations, while clearing thick forests for planting cotton . . . carrying heavy loads of it for hundreds of miles to the market centres monopolized by Portuguese and foreign concessionary companies . . . Mozambican unity was born out of toiling together in the deep, hot, narrow and

dust-ridden shafts of the gold, diamond and coal mines. . .
Our national unity was born out of the common experience
of trying to escape together from Portuguese prisons, forced
labour, palmatoria beatings and political persecutions.'⁹
Thus Mondlane laid a firm and healthy basis of unity on
common oppression and exploitation and not on any mys-
tical concepts.

The first Congress, however, devoted itself more to the
practical and pressing tasks of transforming itself into a
national liberation movement rather than defining at that
stage concretely the aims of the movement, or social and
economic policies after independence. Mondlane undoubtedly was aware of these issues but he did not think that
the first conference was the appropriate time to pose these
problems sharply. He also was feeling his way, for prior to
this, attempts were made by a few leaders of UDENAMO
to disrupt the proceedings by issuing statements that Frelimo was dissolved. The aims of the first Congress according
to Mondlane were summarized as consolidation, mobilization, preparation for war, education and diplomacy. Thus
to develop and consolidate the structure of Frelimo it
sought to promote and accelerate the training of cadres. To
mobilize the population nationally and to give the various
strata organizational direction it sought to encourage and
support the formation and consolidation of trade unions,
student, youth and women's organizations.

Since over 98 per cent of the population of Mozambique
were illiterate, item seven laid down the task to promote at
once the literacy of the Mozambican people by creating
schools wherever possible. This was part of the more important programme of accelerating the training of cadres who
were designated to play a leading role in the politicization of
the masses for the struggles planned for the future.

Like other nationalist organizations, Mondlane recognized that the African liberation movements had a common
enemy, namely imperialism and national oppression, and
therefore their struggles were interconnected. Hence in its
aims Frelimo said it would cooperate with nationalist organizations of the other Portuguese colonies as well as cooperate

27

with nationalist movements of all countries. However from the point of view of the direction that Frelimo was taking, clause 14 was crucial for it proclaimed that the aim of Frelimo was to procure all requirements for self-defence and resistance of the Mozambican people.

The clause made the road that Frelimo was bent on taking crystal clear. The national Front was formed for the purpose of waging an armed struggle. Not all the leaders present believed that this would be realized, and if embarked upon, that they would join in this phase. If they supported the resolution it was because they believed that it would be just a paper resolution. But Mondlane and those around him were serious. For while the Conference was taking place an advance party of cadres, who were later to join Frelimo, had already made its way to Algeria and other places for military training.

If the history of the national movements is written for the whole continent of Africa, it will be found that the people of Mozambique were among the last to form their national organization. In South Africa for instance, the African National Congress (ANC) was formed as early as 1912. In Zimbabwe and Namibia, ZAPU (Zimbabwe African People's Union) and SWAPO (South West African People's Organization) had made their appearance in 1958 and 1960 respectively. In Angola at the time of the founding of Frelimo the armed struggle which the MPLA (Popular Movement for the Liberation of Angola) had begun was already one year old.

But such is the unevenness of historical development that the people of Mozambique were able to process several decades into just one or two years. The Mozambicans were able to combine the formation of the national Front with the launching of the armed struggle. The first shots were fired two years later, but the decision on armed struggle was taken at this historic Frelimo Conference in September 1962.

The establishment of a national Front was itself a momentous stride when the particular realities of the situation in Mozambique are understood. Unlike South Africa and Zimbabwe which have a few large tribes resulting in the languages of the people thus being understood by others, Mozambique had 70 tribes, each speaking a different dialect or language. Few of these languages had been expressed in writing as for example in South Africa; hence there is little written literature of the people in their own language. In fact it is because of this, that Mozambicans in order to be understood by each other, have to use Portuguese. However these differences were overshadowed by a stronger political and economic bond of common oppression.

Frelimo was among the last of the national liberation movements to form a national political organization, but its decision to launch armed struggle at the same time put it into the front line of the liberation struggle in southern Africa. By doing so the people of Mozambique had made a leap, for in that one year they had traversed a road which had taken others decades. In 1962 some still had to commit themselves to this road, while others still had to fire their first shots.

In both these crucial matters, that is the formation of the Front and the decision to launch the armed struggle, one sees the guiding hand of Mondlane. He had stated earlier that he would have no truck with any organization which would be less than a national Front. On the other hand he did not think that the time was ripe to launch a peasants and workers party committed to socialism. In fact, such a move at that time would not have been correct, for the historical conditions were unsuited for it. However, as events later showed, the class struggle manifested itself. But by that time the cadres, who had grown in the struggle and had become politicized, had clear ideas as to the direction of the Mozambican national movement. Thus a broad national Front at that time correctly reflected the aspirations of the people.

There are leaders of workers parties in the national Fronts who take the road of revolution from an understanding of the fundamental laws of society which reveal antagonistic contradictions which can only be resolved by the overthrow of the capitalist system. Hence they take the road of armed insurrection as in October 1917 in Russia, or the People's Wars of China, Vietnam and Cuba. Mondlane

29

arrived at the necessity for armed struggle for a different reason. His experience had showed him that like the Malans and Verwoerds of South Africa, Salazar of Portugal would not budge from his entrenched position. His own experience with South Africa and with other national movements while in the UN showed him that those which took the road of a non-violent struggle ended in a political cul de sac. A non-violent struggle, he had come to recognize, was not the method of struggle suited to the particular conditions of Mozambique. In deciding then to launch an armed struggle, he put Mozambique alongside Guinea Bissau and Angola whose peoples also had taken this road. The result was that other nationalist organizations however much they may have believed in non-violence had no other option but also to take the same road. In the political climate thus created, all the other nationalist organizations of southern Africa were compelled to take the road of armed struggle to achieve independence and freedom.

4

Armed struggle

THE oppressed and exploited workers and peasants in their long and arduous fight for freedom have evolved certain methods of struggle in order to achieve power. One such method was employed by the Bolshevik Party of Lenin. Applying the dictum of Marx and Engels that the class struggle in modern society between the proletariat and the bourgeoisie must lead to the overthrow of the capitalists by the workers, Lenin charted the revolutionary struggle in Russia with this in mind. He politically mobilized the working class which was to play the leading role in the revolution through its vanguard party, the Bolsheviks. When the objective conditions were ripe, when the rulers had lost grip, when the people desired a change, the Bolshevik Party called on the workers and peasants to take power. In October 1917 they did in fact take power and thus ushered in a new phase in the struggle between the exploiters and exploited and between the oppressor and oppressed nations. Power was initially taken in the towns, and later the victory was consolidated in the countryside. The Revolution was swift and the outcome was decided in a matter of days.

Mao Tse Tung proceeded from the same premises. In fact, from the very beginning, he saw that the Communist Party of China was to be a Marxist Leninist Party. And applying Marxism to the concrete realities of the Chinese situation he realized that the Chinese people would have to take the road of a peasant uprising led by the working class. The struggle would take the form of a People's War with its military strategy of guerrilla warfare. It would be a long and protracted struggle, first establishing guerrilla zones, then liberated areas, and then capturing the countryside surrounding the towns and finally the towns themselves. Summing up the Chinese experience, Mao Tse Tung in his 'On People's Democratic Dictatorship' said: 'We have had much valuable experience. A well disciplined party armed with the theory of Marxism-Leninism, using the method of self-criticism and linked with the masses of the people, an army under the leadership of such a party, a united front of all revolutionary classes and all revolutionary groups under the leadership of such a party – these are the three weapons with which we have been able to defeat the enemy.'[10]

This strategy was responsible for the victory in China as well as in Vietnam and Korea and has had wide relevance elsewhere, particularly in the colonies where the working class is not concentrated in any branches of industrial production. The weak link in the colonies for the colonialists is the countryside, and it is here that they have faced defeat. Vietnam however achieved victory applying both the Russian and Chinese roads. In 1945, victory was won through using the Leninist method of armed insurrection. Later, Vietnam won a second victory through a People's war with guerrilla warfare as its military strategy. This road has not resulted only in the expulsion of the oppressors, but also to the final elimination of the exploiters and the establishment of a socialist state.

However, before the oppressed in the Portuguese colonies resorted to armed struggle, one last attempt was made by the advocates of non-violence to dissuade them from taking this road. A Conference was held in Delhi by the Council for Africa based in India. Representatives from Mozambique, Angola and other liberation movements participated. Morarji Desai, at that time one of the leading members of the Indian National Congress, made an eloquent speech for a non-violent approach to the struggle. This was indeed hypocritical and inconsistent for it was just then that the Indian Congress had decided to use armed struggle as the only means to liberate Goa from Portuguese domination. But this line was opposed by the representatives from Africa, and the late Pio Pinto, a socialist from Kenya who was connected with the armed struggle of the peasants against the British, summed up the feelings of others when he said: 'We would like to use non-violent methods, but when you are faced with a régime that refuses to listen to our pleas, then there is no alternative but to use force.'

There was another reason why Mondlane rejected the non-violent method of struggle as unsuitable for the Mozambican people. He saw close similarity between the régimes of Salazar and the Nationalist Party government of South Africa. He had seen organizations like the Indian National Congress and African National Congress using passive resistance of the sort involved in the Defiance Campaign and it had led nowhere. The Mozambican Revolution was indeed fortunate that it had no real history of passive resistance and other forms of non-violent struggle. Hence there was no tradition amongst the people except that of armed struggle. What Mondlane did was to give the people's aspirations of an armed confrontation a vehicle, that is a national organization, and a goal to strive towards.

Mondlane realized that another weapon of struggle which workers have used in their fight against exploitation, namely the strike, would in itself not bring about freedom for Mozambique. He did not rule out strikes altogether. In fact at a certain stage they could be resorted to again, but only as an auxiliary to the main struggle. However, it must also be recorded that the non-violent struggle of the workers in the Portuguese colony of Mozambique has been a glorious and a noble one. Many of them participated in the mighty strike of the gold mine workers on the Witwatersrand in 1946. Like their fellow African workers in South Africa they were not allowed to form trade unions, for only white trade unions were recognized. However, it was the experience of this historic strike that found its ripples in Mozambique a year later. Mondlane says that: 'In 1947 the radical discontent of the labour force, combined with political agitation, produced a series of strikes in the docks of Lourenço Marques and in neighbouring plantations.'[11] It led to an abortive uprising in Lourenço Marques in 1948.

Like the South African fascists who do not hesitate to use the gun to kill and the bayonet to drive the workers into the pits, Salazar's police and army were ruthless and merciless. Not only were the offenders dismissed, but hundreds were sent to the Portuguese Alcatraz to be beaten, tortured, killed or just allowed to rot and die. A further strike took place again in 1956 and here 49 workers were shot down in cold blood. These were heroic sacrifices, but in vain, for this method of struggle in itself would not bring about the desired end. But it was after 1962 that Mondlane recognized that the emphasis had to shift away from the town to the countryside. He writes that in 1962–3, Frelimo working underground also organized a series of strikes. These broke out in Lourenço Marques, Beira and Nacala. The result was the same as in 1947–8 and 1956, with even more savage reprisals, shootings and killings. Mondlane sums up his experience and view of this form of struggle when he says: 'Its failure and the brutal repression which followed in every instance have temporarily discouraged both the masses and the leadership from considering strike action as a possible effective political weapon in the context of Mozambique.'[12]

Armed struggle as Mondlane saw it was to be in the form of a People's War with the military strategy of guerrilla warfare. He did not however formulate it in that way. But he realized that the Russian method of taking power was not applicable to the concrete situation of Mozambique. He wrote: 'The urban population of Mozambique amounts to less than half a million (total population then was seven million). A nationalist movement without firm roots in the countryside could never hope to succeed.'[13] It was in the countryside then, particularly in the northern provinces of Cabo Delgado and Niassa that preparations were made for the launching of the armed struggle.

Two fundamental questions connected with the launching had to be tackled. First, there was the question of the political mobilization of the masses, and secondly the military training of the cadres. These were urgent, and inter-connected. Both were regarded as top priority in the ensuing years until September 1964 when the first shots were fired inside Mozambique. In the early sixties many of the African countries had achieved independence, and one or two like Algeria through armed struggle. The government of Ben Bella agreed to train batches of Mozambican cadres and by 1964, 250 had already received basic military training. It was these who blazed the way right into Mozambique gun in hand, armed also with the conviction that their fight was a just one and that victory one day would be theirs. Heading this group was Filipi Magaia, who became chief of Defence and head of the guerrilla army. He was the first of Frelimo leaders to die in battle. Mondlane in paying tribute at the second Congress said of this brilliant commander: 'Despite Comrade Magaia being absent from Africa when Frelimo Central Committee decided to launch an armed struggle, it was he who was honoured to head the Department of Defence and Security and he brilliantly led the war up to his death. ... I ask the comrades to stand up in memory of Comrade Magaia.'[14] On the military-political plane, the other person that Mondlane paid tribute to was Samora Moises Machel. He said: 'The other Mozambican militant whose contribution merits special mention is the present leader of the Department of Defence, Samora Moises Machel, who directed the politico-military training camps. The political line and military discipline which Comrade Samora was able to inculcate in the fighters is instilled in the

34

life of the Mozambican guerrillas who now serve as the basic elements of the national liberatory struggle without which perhaps our struggle would not have proceeded as such during the latter three and a half years.'[15] Little did Mondlane realize that he was in fact nominating his successor who was to become the President of Frelimo.

It was clear that the emphasis on political mobilization as a prelude to the launching of the armed struggle showed that Mondlane, having absorbed the positive experiences of the Chinese, Vietnamese and Korean revolutions, was going to apply them to Mozambique. The nucleus of the armed forces which was to be the future Liberation Army would not be something operating and fighting divorced from the people. When the trained cadres came back, they would have to live and become an integral part of the nation. But the people themselves had to be educated as to the nature of the struggle, and what the armed forces were fighting for, and against whom. That is why the political mobilization of the people proceeded side by side with military training of the cadres. In particular, attention was paid to the two northern provinces of Cabo Delgado and Niassa. He writes: 'Almost all those who had gathered in Dar es Salaam to form Frelimo were part of the underground forces working inside Mozambique. The three parties which had merged members in various districts and regions and these together with NESAM (Nucleo dos Estudantes Africanos Secundarios de Mocambique), a student organization with which he was associated, and the people who had taken part in the abortive cooperative movement in northern Mozambique formed the basis of the organization which had to be expanded and consolidated. Through this, the aims of the Party had to be explained to the population; the people had to be organized into cells, the general level of political consciousness raised, the activity of the cells coordinated. This was done by underground workers using pamphlets and "bush" telegrams as aids.'[16]

The Frelimo propagandists did not have years of training in political organizations. Neither was there any ideological struggle between correct lines and incorrect lines. That was to come later. But the political ideas imparted were basically sound. What mattered also to the people were that those cadres and militants who came back were their own sons and brothers – and military training had transformed them from awkward youths who knew little about the world, to men who now knew what they wanted. They inspired in their fathers, brothers, sisters, uncles and aunts the confidence that the Portuguese colonialists could be fought. The message they brought from their organization, Frelimo, whose name they had begun to hear frequently, was that they should all help to fight the Portuguese oppressors. It told them that freedom was possible if they all stood together and fought together. In the case of Frelimo, as with other revolutionary organizations, political consciousness grew as a result of active participation and involvement in the struggle, first in the preparation and later in the launching. Therefore in the first phase political mobilization was limited to essential things. In the situation this was what mattered.

For a guerrilla movement to operate for any length of time successfully, it is necessary to have a reliable base area. Strategists of guerrilla warfare regard it as of vital importance. Thus in his 'People's War and People's Army', Giap writes: 'One cannot speak of the armed struggle and the building of the revolutionary armed forces without mentioning the problem of the rear. This is an important problem of strategic significance and a decisive factor to the outcome of the armed struggle and in the building of the armed forces.'[17] Base areas for the liberation struggles engaged in guerrilla warfare have been provided to some extent by independent African states. The NLF of Algeria had its base area in independent Morocco while the Angolan MPLA has used Congo Brazzaville. In the case of Guinea Bissau, Sékou Touré has allowed Guinea to be used. In the case of Frelimo, President Nyerere had already suggested that Tanzania could be used for this purpose. Should Botswana one day be persuaded to allow the freedom fighters the same facilities, there is little doubt that this would accelerate the armed guerrilla struggle in South Africa. Mondlane took up the offer knowing only too well what was involved for Tanzania. He acknowledged the Mozambican people's indebtedness to President Nyerere and the people of Tanzania when he said: 'To follow up this training, coordinate the groups and prepare them to fight inside Mozambique, it was necessary to find a country close by the area of prospective fighting which would permit us to establish at least one camp on its territory. It should be stressed that this is a very serious matter. Any country which agrees to become host to such a military force, even temporarily, must face considerable problems. First is the internal problem posed by the presence of an armed force which is not directly under the country's control. Then there are the diplomatic and security difficulties to be faced. ... Thus when Tanganyika agreed to help us, it was taking a very courageous step.'[18]

What he did not say, but what is known generally is that those countries which allow the freedom fighters to operate within their midst like Guinea, Congo Brazzaville and Tanzania have been subjected to the bombardment of their villages, or acts of aggression by the Portuguese.

Looking at the matter retrospectively it can be said that the launching of the armed struggle after two years of preparation saved Frelimo. It has been the lot of freedom fighter organizations with headquarters outside their countries to be involved in serious bickering and splits, some ideological, but others born out of frustration and loneliness. In these internecine conflicts with harsh polemics degenerating into personal vendetta, there have been cases where factions have used arms and grenades against each other, which were meant for the oppressor. In such cases it is easily understood that factions can easily be manipulated by Western powers whose main aim is to subvert and destroy the national liberatory movements. At the founding Conferences, a great deal of enthusiasm and optimism is generated which rouse the noblest of passions elevating the participants to resolve that they would be prepared to sacrifice all they had. But after the Conference, some sink back into lassitude, and petty jealousies and rivalries get the better of them. This cannot be avoided in a movement which is young, and where love for the cause and devotion for the struggle is not sometimes as strong as the attachment for this or that personality, or advancement of one's own personal career.

Three political groups founded Frelimo and it was expected that there would be disappointments for there could only be one President for Frelimo and one Secretary for the Organization. Thus there were some disgruntled elements. Mondlane mentions one such instance, for, 'when the former President of Udenamo failed to get support for his candidacy for the Presidency of Frelimo, he left Tanganyika and from a foreign African country he announced the dissolution of Frelimo, calling for the formation of a new front. But since he was speaking only for himself and a couple of other disgruntled followers, he did not get any support. He kept floating from one African country to another arguing that Udenamo was not within Frelimo.'[19]

Mondlane shrewdly realized it would not be learned arguments that would decide these issues but active involvement in the struggle. To prevent Frelimo being splintered into its constituents, he set about energetically preparing for the armed struggle. He knew that when people who worked together for a common cause met and discussed common problems then this would weld them together and push to the background differences of tribe, or language. He understood only too well that Frelimo had within it the seeds of its own destruction unless a proper direction was given. 'The heterogeneous nature of the membership carried certain dangers as well as advantages. We came from all over Mozambique and from all walks of life: different language and ethnic groups were represented, different races, different religions, different social and political backgrounds.'[20] However, working and later fighting together created more and more bonds of solidarity, and in this way the different groups were welded together into a national whole. When voices of dissension did appear amongst certain strata of intellectuals and those taking the capitalist road of development, Frelimo had already five years of history behind it, three years of which were in the armed struggle.

The long awaited and historic day for the Mozambican Revolution turned out to be the 25th of September 1964. The terse announcement which has meant so much to this oppressed and downtrodden people, was in fact also a turning point from which there could be no return and was issued by the Central Committee of Frelimo. It read: 'Mozambican People – In the name of all of you, Frelimo today proclaims the general armed insurrection of the Mozambican people against Portuguese colonialism and for the attainment of complete independence of Mozambique.'

The armed struggle was by way of guerrilla warfare, and Frelimo armed forces struck simultaneously at different points in the northern province of Cabo Delgado. The engagements necessarily small in nature were however over a wide area. It is not possible to give all the reports but one will suffice as an example: 'We camped near the lake of the Chai. I told one of our comrades who was in uniform to put on civilian clothes, to go out and reconnoitre the township ... he got into conversation with an African who unknowingly revealed where the troops slept. The white troops slept behind the house of the chefe do posto. The officials slept in the chefe do posto's house. The African soldiers slept in the secretariat. I made a plan for the attack. One machine gun would neutralize the African troops in the Secretariat. I decided to concentrate the attack against the house where the chefe do posto and the officials were. The guard was white. I approached to attack him. My shots would be the signal for the comrades to attack. When he heard the shots, the chefe do posto opened the door and came out – he was shot and killed. Apart from him six other Portuguese were killed in the first attack ... on the following day we were pursued by some troops, and by that time we were far away and they failed to find us.'[21]

In these simple but graphic words, we have an account of the first combat launched by a Frelimo unit, which was one of several on that dark day for Portuguese imperialism. Like the reported one, others followed a similar pattern and by and large Frelimo soldiers got away. The first encounter in anything is the most difficult. It is more so with battle when those trained now have to be put to the test. In the encounter described there were many possibilities which could have frustrated the plan. For instance it was just by chance that the guerrilla unit was given the sleeping places of the Portuguese. But then in war there are chances to be taken. Sooner or later the people would become skilled in guerrilla warfare, for, as the saying goes, one can only learn to swim by swimming. The same is true of war. One could learn all the military theories of war, one could learn to handle all the sophisticated weapons of war, but in the end one can only learn about war by engaging in war itself. The first encounter will reveal all the many problems connected with the struggle and demolish any wrong conception held by the combatant. Reality is seldom interpreted correctly in the first encounter. The brave ones overestimate their own strength and underestimate that of the enemy, while the cautious ones overestimate the enemy's strength and underestimate their own. However it was not insignificant that the commander of this unit chose to take on the most difficult assignment and took as his target the white sentry. In shooting him he also exploded another myth, that the Portuguese were super human and could not be killed. His inexperienced soldiers certainly took heart when they saw that the Portuguese soldier was just like themselves – a human being who can kill and be killed in battle.

One of the reasons for the success of D-Day, that is the 25 September 1964, was that it caught the enemy completely off guard. Guerrilla warfare has no fixed battle lines, no boundaries and no entrenched fortresses. The guerrillas strike in the most unexpected of places. The Portuguese were expecting attacks on the military posts along the frontier with Tanzania. They had underestimated Frelimo strength and its work, for the attacks were launched deep into the interior, some hundreds of miles from the frontier.

The eventful day of 25 September 1964 was also significant for Frelimo in another way. It proved the correctness of the road of a People's War with its military strategy of guerrilla warfare against which the colonialists and aggressors have no real defence. Here after decades of struggles which ended in failure, was one which was able to inflict heavy losses on the enemy without very much loss of life in the people's army. Further, unlike the past struggles where after the defeat, the Portuguese wreaked vengeance on the leaders, here they were powerless, for none could be found. The successful combat boosted the morale of the participants. The Portuguese were not invincible. With correct political ideas and with correct development of military science based on the People's War, the Portuguese could be defeated and victory achieved even if the struggle was protracted.

5

Growth of the armed struggle

It was in 1968 almost four years after the launching of the armed struggle that Mondlane addressed the students of Oxford University on the national liberation struggle in Mozambique. He outlined the early movements, prior to the founding of Frelimo. Of the latest developments of the struggle he said: 'By August 1967, Frelimo's forces had expanded from the original 250 to 8,000 trained and equipped men and women, with many more only lacking equipment. After consolidation, they have been pushing slowly forward and now occupy areas in the north, comprising one fifth of the territory.' What this meant to the people living in these areas was explained by him: 'About one seventh of the population live in areas which are virtually under the control of Frelimo forces. The people are participating in the construction of a new kind of society.' In the rural areas, there was a radical transformation in the system of agriculture in the liberated areas of Cabo Delgado and Niassa. Production was being organized along the lines of a cooperative basis, the result of which was that the Mozambican peasants were able to produce a surplus to pay for essential items such as clothes and tools.

At this meeting he also explained what this new life meant in terms of overall economic and social development. Citing figures which certainly impressed his audience, he said: 'In 1966, 500 tons of cashew nuts, 100 tons of sesame and

41

ground nuts, and ten tons of castor oil seed had been sold. In 1967, 100 primary schools had been started in the Cabo Delgado Province educating about 10,000 children. New schools have been opened in Niassa, where ten teachers have started to educate 2,000 children. No secondary schools have been started yet but in 1963, the Mozambique Institute was established in Dar es Salaam. It has 130 pupils and part of its function is to train health staff for the liberation areas where in the past two years, over 100,000 people have been vaccinated against smallpox.'

What Mondlane showed in his address was that a qualitative change had taken place in the character of the Mozambican struggle. From a military angle he showed the growth of armed forces operating from units of ten to 15 to battalion and even regimental strength. Thus he said: 'On 25 September 1964 Frelimo had only 25 to 250 men trained and equipped who operated in small units. Towards the middle of 1965 Frelimo forces were already operating with units of company strength and in 1966 the companies could operate in battalion strength if required.' By 1967, besides the 8,000 armed guerrilla soldiers which have been mentioned, there were also people's militia and trained recruits who were not yet armed. The enlargement of the people's defence forces showed also in the corresponding increase in the people's involvement in the struggle.

In other words what had begun as a guerrilla operation militarily had slowly become transformed into a People's War. If some of the people at the beginning of the operations were still hesitant, the subsequent action by the Portuguese soldiers made them make up their minds. Since the colonialists could not catch the guerrillas, they sought revenge on the civilian population. The aim was to terrorize them by acts of savagery and barbarism so as to root out any idea of support for the 'terrorists'. The Portuguese authorities thus ordered its military to raze to the ground the people's huts, confiscate their crops if reaped, and destroy those which were on the fields. All the schools were ordered to close down and the hospitals and clinics were placed under the control of the army.

These acts of savagery and vandalism far from cowing the people had just the opposite effect. It opened their eyes to the fact that under Portuguese rule there can be no justice. They were made to suffer, and what they had built up by dint of their sweat and labour had been razed to the ground. And all these hardships and punishment were being inflicted on them although they had committed no crime. Those who lost were embittered. The Portuguese made the same mistake as the Americans in Indo-China of regarding all the nationals as freedom fighters and of treating them as such. These senseless outrages perpetrated by the Portuguese against innocent people educated the people more than any school or university. They had to decide whether to live under Frelimo or the Portuguese. The people had realized that the Portuguese were not prepared to listen to any of their protests however legitimate and pressing they may have been. To illustrate this, it is relevant here to deal with the case of what happened to the people of Mueda. This ghastly incident took place in 1960.

Mueda is situated in the province of Cabo Delgado. The leaders of the people there had brought to the attention of the administration the people's request for more liberty and more pay. This was too much for the chefe do posto, the administrator. He sent word to the people of the area that they should be at Mueda on a particular day to listen to the words of the Governor. Nothing was said about the subject which was to be discussed. But people believed that one of the items would be independence. On 15 June 1960, Mueda was full of people. The Governor arrested Kibiriti and Vanomba whom they believed to be the ring leaders. The Governor asked the gathering: 'Is there anyone who wants to repeat the demand made by these two?' An eye witness to this now relates: 'Immediately hundreds of us stood up, but the governor selected only ten who were allowed to enter the building. Some policemen approached and put handcuffs on Kabiriti and Vanomba. The police were ordered to beat up the ten arrested Mozambicans. . . . All this was done before the eyes of the assembled crowd. When the ten were being taken to the jeep the people advanced. Armed policemen

43

placed themselves in front forming a barrier. They had guns fixed with bayonets ... the Governor tried to run away ... we caught him and began beating him. At that moment the policemen fired on us. They did not shoot in the air – but directly on us. The people started running away; the firing did not stop – on the contrary it increased. Other troops came in and we were caught between two lines of fire, hundreds of people fell. ... I saw myself running over dead bodies until I arrived near a grave. ... I saw things that I shall never be able to forget. For example, under the jeep there were some people who had taken refuge there. I saw the Portuguese police putting their guns under the vehicle and killing them all – one by one.'[22] The people themselves were unarmed, and it is estimated that about 600 people were shot and killed in cold blood.

If Cabo Delgado then was the first province to be liberated, it is to some extent due to the brutal massacre of the people of Mueda, just as gruesome and bloody as Sharpeville, the news of which spread to the whole province and incensed the population. Many now realized that the only road open to them was that of armed struggle.

The rulers face a contradiction when confronted by an awakening population. Either they have to accede to the people's demands and grant independence, or shoot as they did in Mueda. The wiser and far sighted ones in Britain and France decided to withdraw politically in order to enslave them economically all the more. But the Portuguese opted for the opposite course. They stuck on and hence they faced an armed revolt. They believed that by murder, massacre and terror they would be able to terrorize the people into submission. But this had just the opposite effect. It made them more determined to continue. Instead of diminishing, the resistance continues and those few who began the struggle now find their numbers swelling into thousands, tens of thousands and even millions. This is what is happening in Mozambique and in other countries. A Frelimo attack on the Portuguese always invites reprisals. Innocent men and women suffer and are shot, their houses burnt and their crops destroyed. The people are left with no alternative but to side with the resistance actively. A People's War is the result. This fundamental change means that a mighty force which had been damned for centuries is now released. The people become the vast ocean giving forth powerful currents and tides, which no reactionary rulers however fearful and frightening their military strength, however seemingly impregnable their fortifications are able to withstand.

Mondlane understood that a revolution which is protracted is not just a game of chess. It is serious, and in Mozambique the struggle was to be a long one. Unlike the game of chess, real lives are involved and no one is to be regarded as a pawn. Here there is no room for dilletantes who wish to use the struggle to test their pet theories. A heavy responsibility rested with him as well as on the Central Committee of Frelimo to ensure that the basic strategy and tactics were correct, leading to the achievement of their objectives, and not involving unnecessary loss of life. Mondlane was justly proud that the movement of which he was a founder had through the participation in armed struggle begun to grow in political maturity. The military victories, though local in character, were giving the participants and the militants greater and greater confidence.

He knew that the revolutionary struggle would be long and protracted, and therefore he had to fight against two dangers. First, there was the tendency to war weariness on the part of certain African countries which were tired of giving support, and therefore wanted a quick and a decisive victory. Internally too there were some who did not recognize the nature of the war, and wanted to celebrate independence and taste its fruits too quickly. He understood that whether one liked it or not, the war would be protracted but that it would have this redeeming feature in that this would lay a more solid foundation for the future. It would involve more and more people, and it would create a leadership which would grow politically with the revolution. In other words, the People's War would generate a leadership which would have matured with the revolutionary struggle, a leadership which would pursue the revolution to its logical end. And it is the knowledge and understanding of this truth which gave him the optimism which inspires revolutionary leaders. They know that final victory rests with the people.

6

Problems of the Mozambican revolution

THE basic problem of the Mozambican Revolution as well as of other revolutions in the national democratic phase, is who should belong to it, and who should lead it? The Mozambican Revolution developed by way of a National Front, adopting the strategy of guerrilla warfare. Other revolutionary movements faced with situations peculiar to their respective countries have also evolved the idea of a National Front. Mao Tse Tung writes, when China was faced with an attack by Imperialism spearheaded by the Japanese invasion that the task of the Chinese Communist Party, 'is to form a revolutionary national united Front, by combining the activities of the workers, peasants, students, petty bourgeoisie, and the national bourgeoisie throughout the country.'[23] Mao Tse Tung at that time opposed the policy of what he called 'closed doorism'.

In Vietnam, French imperialism, in order to rob the people of their hard won victory achieved by the 1945 insurrection, began to invade the country in 1947. It was then necessary to unite the whole nation and all the revolutionary classes and patriotic elements into a united Front. The Vietnamese Workers' Party put forward the slogan: Unity, Unity and broad Unity — success, success and great success, which became a great reality. Ho Chi Minh's appeal was: 'All Vietnamese, regardless of age, sex, creed, political tendency and nationality must stand up to fight the French colonialists and save the country. Those who have guns must use guns, those who have swords, use swords, and those who have no swords use picks, shovels and sticks. Everyone has to do his utmost against the colonialists to save the country.'[24] In other words, Ho Chi Minh called for the broadest possible front to embrace the entire nation of Vietnam.

46

First, it is to be noted that the Front was in both instances an anti-imperialist revolutionary front which involved armed resistance by the entire nation. In this respect it was fundamentally different from the electoral fronts formed by worker's parties, with elements of the bourgeoisie, to pursue constitutional processes. In Vietnam it was a question of resistance. The Front was to be led by the workers' party based on the worker-peasant alliance. This posed no difficulty for from the beginning of the national struggle in 1930, there was no other party to claim the allegiance of the Vietnamese. But in China it was different. The national bourgeoisie, the petty-bourgeoisie and the landlords had the Kuomintan and this competed with the Communist party for the leadership of the United Front. This was recognized by Mao Tse Tung when he wrote of the need for the Party to maintain its independence, for: 'it is only by firmly maintaining the National United Front that the difficulties can be overcome, the enemy defeated and a new China built. At the same time, every Party, every group in the united Front must preserve its ideological, political and organizational independence; this holds good for the Kuomintan, the Communist Party or any other group . . .'[25]

And on the relationship of classes in the Front he said: 'The same is true of the relationship between the class struggle and the national struggle. It is an established principle that in the war of resistance everything must be subordinated to the interests of resistance. Therefore the interests of class struggle must not conflict with the interests of the war of resistance. But classes and class struggloo are facts and those people who deny the fact of class struggle are wrong. We do not deny the class struggle; we adjust it.'[26]

Thus not only did the Communist party maintain its independence in the Front, but also saw to it that it did not abandon the class struggle. In fact the policy of the Party in the Front was really unity on the one hand, and on the other hand struggle against Japan in the National Front.

The three political groups UDENAMO, MANU and UNAMI which formed FRELIMO were not vanguard

47

Parties. They were nationalist groupings which wanted to end the rule of Portuguese colonialism. The national bourgeoisie in Mozambique was really non-existent and the only large landlords were the white colonialists. The Front thus consisted of peasants and workers in the main, with leadership in the hands of the petty-bourgeoisie, that is, the intellectuals. The supreme organ of Frelimo is the 20 man Central Committee. Mondlane says that the basic unit was the cell of members of the locality. In enemy-held territory, the cell would consist of the most politically advanced cadres. This usually worked underground. The policy making body is the Central Committee, but there is no contradiction between it and the military wing, for leading members in the army are also members of the Central Committee. In the case of Central Committee members, there are rules and regulations governing the behaviour of its members and these extend to one's personal life as well. The regulations also extend to the leading cadres. However, Frelimo is a mass organization, for in the liberated areas, membership is open to any person above a certain age.

With the liberation of Cabo Delgado and the Niassa provinces from Portuguese rule, the problem facing Frelimo was the same as in those countries in Africa where the colonial masters had granted political independence. Mondlane says of this aspect, that in the liberated areas in Mozambique, Frelimo is in fact a government operating within its national territory and not a government in exile. In the liberated zone he remarked how the heavy taxes were gone and the repressive administrative machinery abolished. This was rather an optimistic assessment since it was precisely here that the class struggle rose in all its fury; for the administrative machinery, as well as the liberated territory gave play to the rise of classes springing up from the soil of the revolution, whose aim was to change the direction of the revolution. It also found expression in the Party struggles which broke out after Mondlane's death. However, to understand what was taking place it is necessary at this stage to look at the state machinery which independent African countries inherited from the departing imperialist power and its relation to the nationalist Parties fighting for independence.

National movements throughout Africa ranging from TANU to the Malawi Congress Party before independence were people's organizations. These were vehicles which the people, oppressed under colonial administration, used for the realization of their demands. True enough the goals were defined in the most general way so as to ensure national unity. The different sections amongst the oppressed used to interpret these to suit their own particular interests. But despite their ideological limitations, they were still people's organizations and what was more the people regarded them as such.

The colonial oppressors however manifested themselves in their actions through intervention by their organs of state, namely the army, police and the bureaucracy. And therefore when the people fought their oppressors, they fought this coercive state machinery.

The machinery of the state is part of the superstructure and reflects the economic system. Different economic systems have different superstructures and hence different state machinery. The economic system of colonial powers is capitalism and the whole civil service, army police, judiciary, schools, parliament and town councils not only reflect this, but were so instituted as to facilitate the operation of this system, which on the African continent meant exploitation of the people for the benefit of the colonial masters in London, Paris, New York and Lisbon.

The granting of independence did not mean the alteration or the destruction of this state machinery. Rather the opposite was the case. The feature of the post independence period was that the coercive machinery was expanded and not diminished. Some of the newly-independent countries spent as much as 60 per cent to 80 per cent of the budget on the state machinery. The function of the state machinery had not changed. Africans were performing the very functions which hitherto had been carried out by the whites. This was done in the name of the people.

The Party leaders now became the heads of government

departments. Those cadres of the lower ranks became part of the administrative machinery. This was deadly. It wrecked the Party machinery and in many instances turned an instrument of liberation into an instrument of oppression. First, there was to be fusion between Party and government, and the people were made to believe that they were one. It was no fusion, but absorption, with the Party leaders becoming absorbed into the state machinery, that is the very state machinery which was designed to oppress and exploit the people for the sake of capitalists.

It is not surprising then that in the post independence period, the Party began to wilt and die, for it lost contact with the people at grassroot level. The only time the Party was revived was at election time, when the people were asked to give the leaders the opportunity to continue to run the state machinery.

The Party thus ceased to represent the interests of the people and served the interests of the small indigenous bourgeoisie and the small petty-bourgeoisie. Party officials had become the new privileged group and behaved like rulers. And if they did so, it was because they were performing these very functions, in the name of the people. The gap thus began to widen between the leaders and the people. The leaders were seen as the new foremen of the imperialists.

It is only now after many coups, when progressive governments have been overthrown, that an examination is beginning of the state machinery to analyse its complex workings and to see how imperialism has been using it to entrench itself. It is only now beginning to be understood that the policy of no politics in the civil service in fact serves the imperialists, for in disarming the people politically, the rulers rob them of their vigilance and hence make it easier to carry out a reactionary coup.

The civil service is an institution inherited from colonialism, and it reflects the values and priorities of imperialism. Hence, the tradition of so-called political neutrality is a misnomer, and if carried out by civil servants means the acceptance by them of the imperialist purposes which this institution, like all other colonial institutions, was created to protect and promote.

The lessons that radical leaders of independent African states are realizing is that it is not enough to Africanize the state machinery, the paramount task is to democratize it. This would mean cleaning up and turning upside down for critical examination the whole structure to see just what portions should be incorporated into the new government machinery, and what form it should take. The state machinery has become the breeding ground for not only capital accumulation, but also for power and privilege. Radical governments are now seeing the need to dismantle this machinery and decentralize it, so that instead of power being utilized in the name of the people, from the centre, the people actually have power.

Therefore Mondlane was faced here with a question of a whole overhauling of a state machinery and its critical examination in relation to where it serves the needs of the people, and where it is superfluous. It was not enough, on liberating an area to remove the oppressive taxes which the Portuguese rulers had imposed on the people. This itself was progressive, but inadequate. The state machinery to be consistent with the ideals of the revolution has to be democratized, with power being given to the people. At the same time a proper ratio must be established between the producers and the administrators.

One of the most important reasons for the ideological struggle which broke out in Frelimo after Mondlane's death was that certain leaders of the Front had become part of the state machinery and had used their positions as administrators to exploit the people, thereby enriching themselves.

Mondlane claimed that in the liberated zone, the various systems of exploitation had been abolished; the heavy taxes had gone and the repressive administrative machinery had been destroyed. It was clear that he was looking at the problem from the angle of the state machinery as administered by the Portuguese rulers. Because of the lack of understanding of these issues at the time it was not appreciated that Mozambicans stepping into the shoes of the departing colonial powers could also behave as oppressors. For being in positions of power, they could abuse and misuse it. Only a very politically conscious and well disciplined Party would be able to avoid this pitfall. Frelimo at this stage was on the road to such a political consciousness.

Mondlane at times referred to Frelimo as a Party. A National Front would be a better description, as its name implies. In the Front there are various classes, who have come together to fight a common enemy. But within the classes there are differences, for one class in the Front would want to oust the Portuguese so that they themselves could step into their shoes, and continue the system of exploitation. On the other hand, the mass of the workers and poor peasants would be opposed to such a state of affairs. The Vietnamese, for example, make it quite clear that their Front is based on the worker-peasant alliance and that it is the interests of these groups that receive first priority over and above other groups. In short, in the new society, there must be no exploitation.

The crisis that broke out after Mondlane's death was basically over the same issue, whether the new Mozambique should be structured on a basis of exploitation, or whether there should be a socialist construction of society.

7

Role of the army

ONE significant feature of the Mozambican national liberatory movement was the rapid growth of the People's Liberation Army. The People's Army was not only the vehicle to bring about the desired goal of freedom, but also stood as a guarantee that the conquests of the people would not be taken away from them. Another feature of the Mozambican Liberation Army is that like those in Guinea Bissau and Angola, it is an army which has grown from the people, owing allegiance to no other power or force but to the people.

To put it differently, this army in the main is a peasant army. And what this means can only be understood properly if it is known just what was the nature of the armies which the newly independent African countries inherited from the colonial powers.

In early society before the appearance of private property which split society and brought about class divisions, the defence of the territory was the duty of all. The producer in society was also its defender, for there was no division of labour. Likewise it was the same in Africa before colonial conquest. Every able bodied person was given military training to stand him good stead in case of war. If it was his duty to defend, it was his right that he should be given that training. The armies thus were people's armies, for they were there to defend the interests of the people. Soldiers had no interest inseparable from the people, for they were the people.

The change, however, came about with the division of society between the oppressor and oppressed, which was part of a larger division of society between the exploited and the exploiters. In the case of Africa after the scramble for colonies at the close of the nineteenth century, when the whole continent was partitioned by the Western European powers, the oppressor and exploiter were one and the same person. The oppressor, in the form of the colonial master not only took away the right of the people to arm themselves, but created an army whose personnel came from the oppressed people themselves, but whose whole role was to protect the interests of the colonial masters. The army's officer corps was so indoctrinated by the new masters that they saw their role as no other than that of protectors of colonialism. The army thus became an instrument apart from the people, whose function was to suppress the people. In other words colonial suppression as well as exploitation was through the army, police, and the civil service which imperialism created from the people themselves, but whose role was to suppress and exploit. The colonial rulers had neither the manpower nor the ability to rule without these agents from the oppressed themselves.

When political independence was granted, imperialism

left behind these army officers and top civil servants, who although African, were accustomed to serve the interests of their former colonial masters.

Imperialism knew that as long as the armies of the newly independent states were headed by those who were trained in Sandhurst, St. Cyr or in other military academies of the West, their interests would remain safe. These together with the top civil servants would act as a balancing force against any political leadership from amongst the national movements which decided to go its own way and pursue a course which would end the imperialist stranglehold of the country. When imperialism felt threatened the army could be brought into play and officers could show their loyalty in a concrete way by engineering a coup. That there was a rash of coups in the sixties showed that imperialist reliance on the leaders of national movements to act as imperialist foremen to look after their interests had failed, and that they had to fall back on their trump card – the military. In this way imperialism believed that it would come back to Africa. A recent imperialist coup, the one in Uganda which ousted President Obote, was carried out by the Commander of the Army, General Amin. There are many other similar examples.

However, imperialist plans have been upset and subject to revision because of the growth of the people's armies in Guinea Bissau, Angola, Mozambique, South West Africa and elsewhere. Frelimo's army increased from 250 men to over 8,000 in a very short space of time. This was not counting trained militia and recruits who bore no arms. Even so, Frelimo increased its fighting strength 32 times over three years. Today at a conservative estimate it numbers over 10,000 men. Apart from the type of army that is now rising on the soil of Mozambique, its base, its loyalties, its battle experience and political outlook, in sheer size alone has become a factor to be reckoned with. And this can only be understood if we compare it with African armies whose officer corps was trained by imperialism, and whose political outlook supposedly remains non political but which in fact means it is committed to the politics of imperialism.

Here are comparative figures of the size of armies in Africa in the period 1967–8.

Country	Size of Army	Country	Size of Army
Egypt	213.000	Morocco	50,000
Nigeria	163,000	Ethiopia	45,000
Algeria	57,000	Congo Kinshasa	38,000
Tunisia	21,000	Sudan	27,000
Ghana	15,000	Libya	15,000
Somalia	12,000	Tanzania	7,900
Guinea	5,400	Uganda	6,700
Kenya	5,400	Senegal	5,900
Ivory Coast	4,500	Malagasy Rep.	4,500
Zambia	4,400	Cameroon	4,400
Liberia	4,200	Mali	3,700
Rwanda	2,800	Chad	2,700
Dahomey	2,300	Congo Brazzaville	2,700
		Niger	2,100

The states of Upper Volta, Sierra Leone, Burundi, Maure-tania, Togo, Malawi, Central African Republic, and Gabon all have armies of less than 2,000 men. On the other hand, Gambia, Equatorial Guinea, Botswana, Lesotho, and Swaziland have no armed forces at all.

It will be seen from these figures that the people's armies of not only Mozambique but Angola and Guinea Bissau are numerically larger than most of the African countries which have been granted independence. And this in spite of the fact that even the poorest African country like Botswana or Lesotho, has economic and financial resources far superior to those of Frelimo in Mozambique. It is no secret that during the years in question, the total amount spent by the Liberation Committee of the Organization of African Unity (OAU), on all the liberation movements in the Portuguese colonies, as well as those in South Africa, Zimbabwe, Namibia and Comoro Islands were just three quarters of a million pounds. That was the sum total of contributions by 40 African states to the liberation of their oppressed brothers. Frelimo had to share this amount with all the organizations recognized by the OAU, together with the expenses and

55

salaries paid to those on the Liberation Committee. The salary structures have been calculated according to the U.N. scale and therefore they are large by African standards. In short what the liberation movements receive financially from the Liberation Committee is really a fraction of their needs. Yet in spite of this, the armies have grown.

The liberation armies differ from the professional armies of the African states in many ways. First, the army like the people are engaged in liberation. The result is that in the people's armies are found the best and noblest from among the population, because by joining up the recruits are prepared to lay down their lives for no other reward than that they may do their duty to free their country from foreign rule. There can be no question of a career in such an army, and there are no privileges, and no pensions or retirement plans. But the guerrilla knows that if he lays down his life, the people through the liberation organization will look after his wife, children and aged parents. In the liberated areas of Mozambique when it comes to the question of the allocation of land, it is the children and close relatives of freedom fighters who receive special consideration. Regarding wages, what the officers in the liberation army are getting is not different materially from the rank and file soldier; and the army as a whole does not live any differently from the people. For what the soldiers receive by way of a wage is not different from what the people receive or obtain through their produce.

On the other hand, if there are no financial inducements to join the army those who are in it are amply rewarded. In the Frelimo army it is possible for anyone to rise right to the top, for the revolution gives scope for its men to show their creative talents, their daring and skill in battle. Thus Mondlane says: 'Leadership is not based on rank, but on the concept of responsibility; the leader of a certain body is referred to as the man "responsible" for it. Many of those now "responsible" had never been to school before they entered the army; they were illiterate, with no formal education, when they joined near the beginning of the war. They have acquired the ability to lead through their practical experience

56

of fighting and political work, and through the education programmes of the army.'[27]

Secondly, the army is self-reliant and Mondlane underscores this when he says that Frelimo forces live off, for the most part, what they produce. This the people appreciate, for the colonial powers only developed the economy of the oppressed people where it would directly serve colonial interests. The result was that the people themselves were not able to produce a surplus. Their economy was kept at subsistence level, while they had to find taxes to pay for the upkeep of the bureaucracy and the army under the colonial power. That is why colonial people view the civil service, the police and the army with hatred, for they see them as a parasitic growth which not only lives off them for they are not engaged in production, but which also controls and oppresses them. Before the colonial period, the army which the people had been used to was one which fought when required, but whose members spent the rest of the time in production.

Here then was a new development on a higher plane. In the people's liberation army they saw a force that not only did not live off them, but was self-reliant as far as possible, and was also there to protect and defend them in case of enemy attacks. In this way, first by relieving the people of the burden of supporting them, and secondly by spreading a protective umbrella over them, the liberation army was able to forge a dynamic unity between itself and the people. This the oppressor armies have never been able to do.

Thirdly, unlike the armed forces of colonial times and those in the post independence period, the people's liberation army was not confined to the barracks. The army was very much part of the people, participating with the people in some of its social activities. Thus Mondlane says: 'The army is helping to raise the standard of education as well as general political consciousness. Recruits are taught wherever possible to read and write and to speak Portuguese. The army also organizes various specific training programmes such as radio work, accounting and typing as well as subjects oriented towards war. Thus the army becomes the people's

57

school as well as their university. In the bush, mountains and the fields, with the sky as the only roof, the "people's schools and universities are springing up".[28]

These are some of the reasons for the phenomenal growth of the army in Mozambique. The people know that Frelimo is their organization and that the army is part and parcel of it. That is why, while the mothers and fathers tend the fields, hoe and reap, they send their children to join the army. They know this invites reprisals from the enemy. They even know that this invites the wrath of the rulers and they could well be arrested, tortured and their shambas razed to the ground. But the people know that there is no other way out; that it is better to stand up and fight, come what may, than to live the life of slaves and doom their children to eternal bondage. This is one of the ways that the people of Mozambique have shown in the most concrete way that they support the struggle of Frelimo.

A force that is becoming increasingly politicized, a force that is part of the people, a force that is self-reliant, a force that is an instrument of struggle and not a haven for career-ists, these are some of the features which distinguish the people's army of liberation in Mozambique from an estab-lished, professional army, and also accounts for its phenom-enal rise in size.

In some parts of Africa, as well as in Asia and Latin Am-erica, a practical problem has arisen as to who should control who. It has become a matter of crucial importance and it has been neatly summed up in the phrase, does the Party control the gun, or should the gun control the Party? Or to put it differently, what is to be the relationship between the Party and the army? Mondlane undoubtedly was aware of the Vietnamese experience as well as the Chinese experience on this matter. Thus for instance Giap in his 'People's War and People's Army' writes: 'Our army is a people's army, the army of the toiling people, essentially of the workers and peasants and led by the party of the working class. It is the armed forces of the people's democratic state, which was formally in essence, the worker-peasant dictatorship and now the proletarian dictatorship. This is the revolutionary and the class nature of our army. This is the basic difference between the enemy's army and ours.'[29]

And in defining what he calls the 'fundamental principles of army building' he says: 'The most fundamental principle in the building of the army is to put it under the party's leadership, and to strengthen the party's leadership of the army. The party is the founder, the organizer and educator of the army ... the system of party committee and political commissar must be maintained.'[30]

Mondlane also knew that with the absence of political consciousness in the forces, or if there was a serious difference in the political leadership, the army elements could well step in and take control. Acknowledging that it was possible for contradictions to develop between the army and the Front, Mondlane says that this is minimized by the fact that both the civilian and military are answerable to the political body of Frelimo. Here of course he was referring to differences that did arise between the civilian wing who were working underground and the military cadres who arrived later in Mozambique. The difference was on the question of the nature of authority. This was settled by Frelimo.

Mondlane said that Frelimo was composed of both military and civilian personnel and that the relationship between the political, military and civilian was not one which could be described in terms of a near hierarchy where one was subordinate to the other. Policy decisions were to be made by the political body, the supreme organ of which was the Central Committee. The army like the various departments worked in conformity with decisions made by the Central Committee, but the army leaders themselves were members of the Central Committee and thus also helped to make policy decisions. The meeting of the military commanders of Frelimo is normally presided over by the President or the Vice-President which ensures that between Central Committee meetings, close coordination between the political and military is maintained. Thus Mondlane said that while it is the political body of Frelimo, that is the Central Committee of Frelimo, which is supreme, there is no contradiction, for leading military men belong to the Central

59

Committee, while the head of the Central Committee presides over the meetings of the Department of Defence.

There are some who argue that because of the low ideological level in Frelimo when the leadership crisis erupted after Mondlane's death, the new President, Samora Machel was chosen solely because he had control of the army. For in the Second Congress he was elected to the Central Committee, for the first time. That may be, but it must be remembered that he belonged to the younger generation of Frelimo leaders and his services and contributions were singled out by Mondlane at the Second Congress.

Like Mondlane, Machel sees no contradiction between Party and army. Interviewed shortly after his election as President of Frelimo, he said: 'War is an instrument of getting political objectives. There is therefore no contradiction between my being President of Frelimo and Commander of Frelimo's army. It just makes it easier to make decisions. Actually, I am neither President nor Commander of Frelimo. The people are.' He added that he travels with the Headquarters 'in his pocket'.

Mondlane was able to assimilate the experiences of the struggles from other countries, particularly those who had and were still waging a struggle similar to theirs. He selected the good, and rejected the bad, the latter in the sense that it was not suited to the concrete realities of Mozambique. An example of this can be seen when he deals with the relationship between the guerrilla and the militia. Unlike some writers on guerrilla warfare he did not see any distinction between guerrilla and the member of the militia. In fact he tried to show that their role was complementary and it was the militia which provided the vital link between the people and the guerrillas. He therefore writes: 'On the local level, in the field, the people's militia plays an important part in linking the civilian population and the army. These militias are formed from the militant members of the civilian population, who carry on with their normal occupations (producers) and, at the same time, though not incorporated in the guerrilla army, undertake certain military duties. Their main task is the defence of their home region . . . While there is

60

fighting in an area, they coordinate their activities with the guerrillas, reinforce them when necessary, and supply them with information about their particular locality. When the guerrilla forces have liberated an area, the militia can then take over the organization of defence, of production and supply, leaving the main forces free to move on to a new fighting area. . . . In regions where there is not yet an active armed struggle militias are formed in secret whose task is to prepare the ground for guerrilla fighting; to mobilize the people; to observe the Portuguese forces, to arrange supplies and assistance for the guerrillas as they move into the region.'[31]

Mondlane concludes on his conception of the role of the militia: 'The people's militia are the backbone of the armed struggle.' In other words, far from dismissing them, Mondlane regards their role not even as auxiliary, but almost of the same importance as the people's liberation army. In this view, he is closer to the Vietnamese and Indo Chinese who regard their role as primary and fundamental.

The emergence of a people's army adopting the strategy of guerrilla warfare and its rapid expansion threatens to alter the balance of power in southern Africa. On the eastern side in Mozambique, and on the western side in Angola, armies are being built over which imperialism has no control, for they use a method of warfare which is very difficult to combat. Imperialist military strategy was based on the concept of building a south African army composed of whites, which with its citizen force and commandoes, would number over 100,000 men. Like the Israeli army it is supposed to be mobile and with the swift striking power. South Africa alone spends over £175 million annually on defence. The armies of southern and central African states look puny by comparison with little or no striking power. If they engaged in conventional warfare, they could easily be crushed.

That is why Vorster says that if he chose to he could over-run most of the neighbouring African states within a few days. And to bolster this up, he cites the case of Israel, which because the Arab armies chose to confront it with conventional methods, found themselves on the defensive

61

because of the mobility and striking power of the aggressor army. On the other hand, Vietnam and Indo China have shown that mobility and fire-power are useless when they have to fight a People's War adopting the military strategy of guerrilla warfare. The U.S.A. which has marshalled the deadliest fire-power known in the history of war has been defeated ignominiously by the Tet Offensive in 1968 and in Laos in 1971. Likewise the Palestinian fedayeen showed the Arab people that there was nothing intrinsically wrong with them. The reason for their defeat was that they had used the wrong ideas, wrong methods and wrong military science in combating Zionism. Within six months they were able by their activities to show up the vulnerability of the Israeli army.

So too in the case of Mozambique. Portugal has a large army of over 60,000 in this colony. It spends over £80 million annually on defence, which is half of its budget, to feed its armies in the three African colonies which are in the process of throwing off its yoke. Portugal is being supplied with the latest NATO weapons. Yet despite that it has not been able to save its two northern provinces in Mozambique. It has engaged in the most savage campaigns of reprisals and repressions. But this has not prevented it from being forced into enclaves. Mondlane recognized the superiority of the method of guerrilla warfare, for against it the rulers and aggressor armies have no defence. He writes: 'Frelimo's forces live for the most part off what they produce in the fighting areas, and what has to be transported is taken on foot through the bush between the small centres which have been established. As a result, Frelimo has no vulnerable supply lines, no military or economic strategic positions to defend. The loss of a single small base or area of crops is not very serious; it has no significance beyond the immediate loss of resouces.'[32]

Mondlane was confident that the very protractedness of the struggle was laying the foundation of a popular and conscious movement for he adds: 'The longer the struggle lasts, the more evident becomes its popular basis, the more support flows to Frelimo ... thus every victory adds to our chances of winning yet further victories and reduces the ability of the Portuguese to counter our activities.'[33]

In Southern and Central Africa, in the liberation armies one sees a growth of people's power resting on armies which belong to them. That cannot be said of most of the African countries which have been granted political independence by the colonial powers. It is this people's power over which imperialism has no control. The People's Liberation Armies in southern Africa are fiercely anti-imperialist for they have grown and developed fighting Portuguese imperialism and its NATO allies.

These armies are popular and democratic in the sense that they spring from the people. By their example and devotion, in protecting the conquests of their revolution as well as advancing it they have shown national movements which received independence through constitutional means what a popular army should do and what role it can play not only in safeguarding independence, but also in furthering the African Revolution. In the coming life and death struggle against imperialism, when there will be confrontation between pro and anti-imperialist forces in Africa, the guerrilla armies with their rich accumulated experience will have an important role to play, for they will not be confronting imperialism gun in hand for the first time.

8

Role of the intellectuals

IN a capitalist society the two dominant classes are the bourgeoisie and the workers, that is, the owners of production and the producers of wealth, the modern proletariat. In Africa we also have a small urban proletariat and the rural proletariat, the landless peasants who work for the capitalists in the large plantations. But sandwiched between the two giant forces lies the intermediate class, the petty bourgeoisie. This consists of small traders, independent handicraftsmen, professional men and layers of the civil service. It is largely from this strata of the petty bourgeoisie that the intellectuals are drawn.

The term 'intellectual' refers to all those who have had secondary or high school education. They include university graduates, teachers, students, priests, and other members of the professional class. Civil servants too, by virtue of their education, could be classed in this category, particularly if they identify themselves with one or other of the social groups. Petty bourgeois elements are also in the communications media, for example in newspapers and radio and television services.

In Africa, the intellectuals have occupied a position of importance far greater than their numerical strength. But that is understandable for in the minds of the people they represented progress and enlightenment. Mondlane's mother told him to go and learn the 'witchcraft' of the white man, so that it could be used to liberate them from oppression. Yet in a sense the intellectuals are a creation of capitalism. With the conquest of Africa, imperialism was faced with the problem of ruling the colonies. In the intellectuals it saw a link between itself and the colonized people. They occupied positions as teachers, priests and civil servants. Since the dominant class in society was the capitalist class, who were also their masters, the intellectual's function was to transmit its ideas, values, and mores to the illiterate masses. For this the rulers paid the intellectuals, and treated them a little above the masses, throwing a few concessions and privileges here and there.

If the rulers used the intellectuals to propagate its ideas to the masses, the people also needed their services. As the only literate section, they were expected to tell the people what was happening in society, and what was being planned against them by the rulers. The people also wanted to know the ins and outs of modern industrial society. The militants and rebels amongst the people also expected the intellectuals to show them a way out to bring about liberation. In the eyes of the people, education meant progress, and therefore although they themselves skimped and starved they saw to it that their sons and daughters were sent to school.

64

Britain in the nineteenth century encouraged the building of schools in her African colonies, for from these would arise the black teachers and priests whose services were needed to bolster up capitalist exploitation. Portugal, however, at that time was a decadent mercantilist state, and made very little attempt to build schools, let alone universities in her African colonies. Rudimentary education was left in the hands of the Catholic Church. Therefore, the generation of Mondlane and those after him had to leave Mozambique if they wanted to pursue studies from secondary school onwards. It was these students who formed NESAM in 1949.

Although the national movement in Mozambique was formed only in the sixties, the intellectual tradition of revolt dates back to the early twenties. In the hey day of Portuguese liberalism there arose the 'Liga Africana' formed in 1920 in Lisbon whose members stood not only for national unity but also Pan African Unity. This group attached itself to the radical elements who were opposed to imperialist plunder of the African continent. However, this was a tiny intellectual group completely divorced from the masses and operating from Lisbon. Their importance lay more in the advanced radical ideas they propounded than in any significant impact they had on Mozambican society. This was followed by the O Brado Group operating from Mozambique who rejected all discrimination based on colour, who demanded equality and the immediate solution of the problem of hunger from which the people were suffering. A younger generation of intellectuals had seen that racial discrimination and exploitation were two facets of the same problem, and that the oppressor and exploiter were one and the same person. Therefore the struggle for national liberation was also a movement to end exploitation. It would be ridiculous to remove the oppressor and then bring him back as an exploiter.

In the forties and fifties there also arose a group of intellectuals who wrote poetry of protest. This was typified by the Craveirinha group. These in their writings denounced the brutality of the colonial oppressor, his barbarity and the attempt to take away from them their manhood, by obliterating their past and making them rootless. In this poetry, full of passion and anger and sympathy for the oppressed, dehumanized and degraded Mozambican, can be seen the germs of the future cultural renaissance of the Mozambican nation.

Mondlane though of peasant stock was then by education and occupation an intellectual. He thus understood their problems well. With the intellectual there was a gap between theory and practice. To identify himself with the people, he had to cut his links completely with the rulers as well as with the capitalist world. That is exactly what Mondlane did, and he tried to get the Craveirinha group to do likewise. If he did not succeed completely with this older group for various reasons, one of which was that they were watched by the PIDE or were in prison, he managed to get the younger group, mostly in NESAM to cast their lot with Frelimo. He writes: 'I myself as one of the students returned from South Africa who had founded NESAM, was arrested and questioned at some length about activities in 1949. Nevertheless, NESAM managed to survive into the sixties, and even launched a magazine, *Alvor*. ... NESAM's effectiveness like that of all the early organizations, was severely limited by its tiny membership. ... But in at least three ways it made an important contribution to the revolution. It spread nationalist ideas among the black educated youth. It achieved a certain revaluation of national culture, which counteracted the attempts by the Portuguese to make African students despise and abandon their own people ... it established a nationwide network of communications ... which could be used by a future underground.'[34] It was through NESAM that Mondlane was able to get cadres who were to form the nucleus of Frelimo.

A national movement or a political party, particularly if the struggle is long and drawn out is faced sooner or later with division. In fact division, that is one divides into two, is a fundamental law of development. However, for division to lead to a split in the organization will depend on a number of factors. Whether the split is deep and irreparable will also depend on whether in the ideological polemics any distinct

66

trends can be observed. In the last analysis, deep fundamental divisions leading to splits can be traced to differences of class interest. However, in the splits it is the intellectuals who prominently figure, for it is they who propound and put forward the ideas of the various class groups.

The three organizations which banded together to form a Front in Frelimo had intellectuals as their leaders. However, apart from small groups, Frelimo was saved from a major split because the intellectuals were to be involved firstly in the preparation of the struggle and later in the struggle itself. This was to prove the real testing ground and to separate the genuine intellectuals who wished to cast their lot with the people and those, who because of their psychological make-up did not believe that the Portuguese could be fought. The climate then in Frelimo was that there was no room for ideological disputes, because everyone was doing something for the struggle. The result was that these leaders quietly dropped out. They did so without any fuss and struggle, without using smokescreens to leave. Frelimo thus was saved from internecine strife. The positions of those who left were taken by others who because younger had grown up in a different political milieu. The strategy then of preparing for the launching of the armed struggle simultaneously with its founding saved Frelimo.

It was only in 1967 that a revolt did break out and it was confined to a certain section of the students who were studying in overseas universities, particularly in the West. This however had its echo in the Mozambique Institute in Dar es Salaam, which at that time was Frelimo's secondary school.

The problem that the dissident students posed to Mondlane was whether they as a group should stand apart from the people, and secondly whether they should be amenable to the discipline of Frelimo. Mondlane's standpoint was that in a population where 95 per cent of the people were illiterate, being a student was itself a privilege. The students in the main were scholarship students, and this was a direct consequence of the armed struggle launched by Frelimo. Frelimo had decreed that all students who had to leave Mozambique for further studies had to participate for a certain period in the struggle and had to perform certain tasks specified by Frelimo. The aim of this was to link the student more to the people and to give him the consciousness to place at the service of the people what he acquired by way of education. The people on the other hand would also be satisfied, because if they were to continue to sacrifice and even give up their lives, they would not like to see those who had done nothing for the struggle move in and reap the benefits. It was this discipline with which the students were unwilling to comply. Students for instance who had qualified for their B.A.s or M.A.s did not wish to interrupt their studies, and insisted on doing further specialization.

The people of Mozambique needed intellectuals but what was to be their political orientation? In his polemic with the students Mondlane said that there was a need for trained leaders, but leaders must be revolutionary. Academically, qualifications of colonialist leaders were often excellent, but they used their knowledge to oppress the people. Mondlane wanted the intellectuals to be trained in the armed struggle. In that way, the poisonous ideas inculcated into the students by the West, that they were superior to the people would be eliminated. It would also do away with the idea that because they were educated they were entitled to privileged social and material positions. Mondlane correctly stated that, the struggle is the most important and best training school there is in the world ... the revolution also needs and cherishes its students, leaders and revolutionary intellectuals, but they can get more of an education in the Revolution than in a university.

In his polemic with the students, he saw that the students were goaded by certain powerful interests and that they received their inspiration from those foreign powers who were opposed to the armed struggle in Mozambique. He thus exposed the whole aim of the Western countries in granting scholarships. He said that socialist countries and various organizations (who give scholarships) show solidarity with our struggle, while the Imperialist countries which collaborate with the Portuguese give scholarships in an attempt to educate a leadership which would be favourable to their side. Even students who had deserted the ranks of Revolution were able to get scholarships and to benefit directly from the Frelimo struggle.

What was to be the correct line in dealing with the intellectuals? Should they be treated as outcasts and driven into the hands of the enemy? On the other hand, should they be allowed to infect the national movement with the ideas of the oppressors and exploiters that they should have a privileged position by virtue of their education? Should they place their own personal interests and interests of their small group above that of the nation?

It must be stated that this problem is not peculiar to Frelimo, or even to the African Revolution. In fact at one time or another, most revolutionary organizations and Parties have had to face this problem. The intellectual, by virtue of his training, is useful to any society, whether capitalist or socialist, and needed particularly by revolutionary Parties. But to be really effective he must be purged of his reactionary ideas which would do harm to the struggle.

In China for instance, the intellectuals were distrusted by sections of the Party and the army. No attempt was made to recruit them and they were debarred from taking responsible posts. Mao Tse Tung, however, issued a directive to the Party from the Central Committee that an attempt should be made to recruit as large a number of intellectuals as possible. This was in December 1939. Noting that: 'many of our army cadres are not yet alive to the importance of intellectuals, they still regard them with apprehension and are even inclined to discriminate against them or shut them out. Many of our training schools are still hesitant about enrolling young students in large numbers. All this is due to the failure to understand their importance to the revolutionary cause. ... Without the participation of the intellectual, victory in the revolution is impossible ... the proletariat cannot produce intellectuals of its own without the help of existing intellectuals.'[35]

Of course, the Party in this case assigned proper and appropriate work to the intellectuals and gave them political education so that in the long course of the struggle they gradually overcame their weaknesses, revolutionized their outlook and identified themselves with the masses. In this way Mao Tse Tung was not only able to preserve the national character of the united Front but also was able to utilize the skills, ability and resources of the intellectuals for the benefit of the Revolution.

In the case of Frelimo it was not a question of shutting them out; on the contrary it was a question of getting them in, and once in to see that they were disciplined like the rest and placed their own interests below that of the nation. The guidelines that Frelimo laid down were that:

1. All students leaving Mozambique to pursue their studies, must participate for a certain period in specific tasks in the struggle for national liberation.
2. Youths over 18 years of age who had not completed primary schooling were to be immediately integrated into the politico-military programme.
3. Youths under 18 years who had completed primary school were to be integrated into the Mozambique Institute to pursue secondary studies up to the second cycle of high school.
4. Other youths approaching 19 years of age attending advanced classes in technical and liberal art schools were to be encouraged to continue their studies in foreign schools.

However, it was made clear that they were to regard themselves as one of the battalions of Frelimo, for the student went abroad because Frelimo decided that this was best, and the student was in a way continuing as a part of a national action.

Mondlane remarked that his polemic with the students was with only a small minority because the student body as a whole agreed with the guidelines and integrated themselves with the people. But his ideological struggle with this section of the intellectuals was a struggle to see that the national movement was not infected with bourgeois individualism and that it retained some degree of discipline both in ideas as well as in actions.

What Mondlane at that time did not know was that there were some elements in Frelimo who had put these minority students in the forefront as a kite, to see what would be the reaction of the rest of Frelimo. For if the students got away with their attitudes and had their own way, then those who were using their positions to exploit the people under cover could also get away.

Mondlane in a spirit of self criticism said that the Frelimo Central Committee itself could have done more to educate the students politically on the aims of the Revolution and the tasks ahead for them. In this way they would not have been a prey to the ideas of individualism that were floating around campuses during this period. They would not then have aspired to special privileges for themselves. Being integrated with the people would have given them a direction and a purpose, and this would have been their anchor against the onslaught of anti-liberation and anti-national ideas.

9

Tribalism

ONE of the major problems facing independent African states as well as national liberation movements is tribalism. It is a singular obstacle retarding the progress towards the building of the nation. As Kwame Nkrumah rightly points out in his recent book 'Class Struggle in Africa'* before conquest there were tribes but no tribalism. But just as imperialism used religion to divide a people who were otherwise culturally one and living as an entity in a nation, so too tribalism has been used for this same purpose. Africa before conquest by capitalism and later by Imperialism was moving towards a stage where tribes were in the process of coalescing

*Panaf Books, 1970.

to form in embryo the nation state. But one of the effects of colonialism and imperialism was to break up the growing bonds of unity between the various tribes. Thus tribes which were coming together to face the European conqueror and aggressor were separated from each other and in many cases turned against each other.

Tribal man is at a certain stage of social and economic development. Out of the tribal society has grown the nation state. Basically a tribal form of society is based on communal ownership of land with chieftainship as its political form of government. The chief is the political head of the tribe, but he is responsible to the people and cannot go against their collective wishes.

With conquest this form of social organization disintegrated and the people became part of the wider world capitalist system based on wage slavery. The economic basis of tribalism was undermined, for with the compulsory payment of taxes, money had to be found. This meant work in the mines, factories and plantations.

While this was so, imperialism saw to it that large areas remained undeveloped with no roads or railways. This encouraged regionalism and parochialism and tribal thinking. The Portuguese like the other imperialists also encouraged tribalism and one way they did this was to preserve some of its features, one of which was chieftainship. The chief now was the agent of his colonial master and because they paid him he had to carry out their orders and instructions. While they left large areas undeveloped, with only a subsistence economy, there were sectors which they incorporated into the world capitalist economy. These were the rubber, cotton, sisal, coffee, tea plantations as well as the tin, coal, gold and copper mines. So on the one hand there was stagnation in large sectors of the economy while on the other hand the rural and urban workers were linked in a network controlled by giant international monopolies. This uneven and lopsided economy was what imperialism left behind when it granted political independence.

With hardly any industrial development, with a poor commercial sector, with an agricultural economy either subsistence or tied to the imperialist world economy, the only other avenue for jobs was the state sector. There was a veritable scramble for the well paid jobs. Many of the educated people could not find jobs and a feature of the newly independent countries is the high level of unemployment amongst the younger generation. Under such conditions it was understandable that tribalism which was fostered under imperialism was brought into play. It was a fight for power, a fight for well paid jobs and the target was the state machinery. Kwame Nkrumah rightly says in 'Class Struggle in Africa' that many of the tribal fights are really different sections of the indigenous bourgeoisie fighting for power and using tribalism as the cover.

Mondlane had already experienced how tribalism was wreaking havoc amongst the newly independent African states. Further, he had seen how Verwoerd had tried to resurrect tribalism in South Africa in order to send the people back into history. He realized that in a modern society there would be no place for either tribalism or chieftainship. In fact, like most radical thinkers he regarded tribalism as a hindrance to progress and that way of life which stood for political and social equality. He also recognized that chieftainship was being perpetuated to maintain colonial domination.

Within two years after the launching of the armed struggle, Frelimo was faced with the problem of administering the liberated territory and therefore it had to formulate a policy as regards chieftainship. What was to be the position of chiefs in the new society that the Revolution was now creating? In 1966 the Frelimo Central Committee came out with a directive. First, those chiefs who had allied themselves with the Portuguese were to be removed from authority and if they had perpetrated any crimes against the people, they were to be punished. Secondly, those who had remained neutral or who had sided with the people were to be allowed to continue for the time being, though 'the progress of revolutionary power has the effect that traditional power gradually fades away'.[36]

One of the principal functions of the chief was the

allocation of land. This was now in the hands of Frelimo and, in any event, with the growth of cooperatives this chiefly function would not be necessary. The cooperative was a higher form of economic organization than anything devised under chieftainship.

The other problem was one of tribal tendencies within Frelimo itself. In 1966 the Frelimo Central Committee had condemned tribalism and regional tendencies shown by certain comrades as being contrary to the interests of the Mozambican Revolution, for it impeded the successful development of the people's liberation struggle. The directive emphasized that the battle againt tribalism and regionalism was as important as the battle against colonialism.

Frelimo is not the only revolutionary organization in Africa which has passed resolutions against tribalism. In some form or other most Parties have passed resolutions condemning it. Not infrequently it has been found that those who denounce tribalism in other leaders are themselves guilty of the same crime. It is tribalism in others, not their own tribalism which they object to. In such cases, we are dealing with the squabbles of certain sections of the indigenous bourgeoisie who are exploiting tribal prejudices to get positions of power for themselves and their particular group.

Mondlane however was above all this. His experience overseas had given him a different outlook and he was able to look at problems nationally and later even from a class angle. He looked at an individual according to what he was worth, what contribution he could make, and was not concerned with his tribe. He set about combating tribalism by increasing the political consciousness of the cadres first, and the people afterwards. However, it was in the army and in the liberated areas that he was able to put his ideas into effect. He writes: 'In the army, people from different areas accordingly mingle, so that each unit contains representatives from different tribes and different areas fighting together. In this way, tribalism is being effectively combated within the forces, and an example is being set to the rest of the population.'[37]

Tribalism cannot be easily rooted out, for it sustains itself in the low development of the productive forces in society. And in large areas of Africa the subsistence economy still prevails. Eradication of tribalism will be a long and a slow process, but what is vital at this stage is that the cadres of the revolutionary movement must, because of their high political consciousness, be in a position to expose those leaders who fan the flames of tribalism for their own selfish reasons. Once the politically conscious section forms a barrier to the dissemination of ideas encouraging tribalism, then the people cannot be confused or misled. And at present the most consistent fighters against tribalism are the people who have been imbued with socialist consciousness. Nationalist ideology itself is not sufficient, for once a nationalist is scratched a little, one often sees a tribalist.

IO

Racialism

RACIALISM is a modern phenomenon connected with the rise and growth of capitalism. At the root of racialism, which manifests itself in racial discrimination, is class exploitation.

Capitalism has used the differences of race, colour and religion to intensify its exploitation of the peoples of Africa and Asia. After the end of the nineteenth century, the industrially advanced countries of the West had completed their conquests of these two continents. The result was that the division between the conquerors and conquered, colonizers and colonized, was also one between the white nations and the non-white nations. To rationalize their domination and their intensified exploitation of non-white peoples, the ideologists of the bourgeoisie put forward the idea of superior and inferior races. And one of the many pernicious ideas propounded was that the black people of Africa had no history, no culture and no civilization comparable to that of the whites. The absurdity of this argument can be seen in that

75

the people of Asia had a history (which they admitted), a civilization and culture, and yet they were as exploited and oppressed as their brothers in Africa. That the people of Africa had no culture and civilization, or no history is a myth, and this has been exploded by the historians of the post independence era.

Another of the insidious techniques employed was to inculcate in the minds of the rising generation of African intellectuals that the whites were superior to the blacks in all fields. The whites represent progress, enlightenment and civilization while the blacks are backward, primitive and uncivilized. Many of the young intellectuals who were impressionable were infected with the slave mentality. Even today after a decade of independence it has not completely worn off. Only a few years ago, African Cabinet ministers were accustomed to rise in deference to their white permanent secretaries. Thus if today Banda of Malawi and Houphouet-Boigny of Ivory Coast are propounding the idea of a dialogue with South Africa it is only because mentally they are still unemancipated, and continue to regard the whites as superior and the blacks as inferior. They also subscribe to the belief that the whites are invincible militarily and any confrontation with them would end in defeat for the blacks. They are therefore prepared to accept the role the whites have allocated to them. The experiences of Indo-China, the very recent case of Vietnam where a small country with a small people is able to defeat the mightiest of the white powers, has not had any effect on their thinking. In their case, the disease of slave mentality has been so insidious that they will die believing that the white man is a kind of God.

Most national movements are faced sometime or another with the problem of racialism. And in Mozambique it was the same. Mondlane was faced with the problem of fighting the disease of slave mentality on the one hand which the Portuguese had instilled that the white man was like a God and could not be killed or defeated. He was so powerful that even bullets could not bring him down. At a later stage in the development of Frelimo another form of racialism also reared its head. This was racialism in reverse which regarded all white men, all the Portuguese as oppressors, independent of their political stand or views.

As regards the first, Mondlane recalls in the early days of the awakening of the Mozambican people, how the student organization NESAM conducted an ideological struggle against the insidious ideas of the Portuguese that the Mozambicans were inferior and that they either had no culture or that their culture was inferior. He showed how in the battle conducted then on the ideological plane the young students put forward the idea of a national culture and of looking at the people of Mozambique not as an appendage of the Portuguese, but as an independent and distinct people. Once they were mentally free, the intellectuals embarked on the next step, the struggle for national liberation.

However, it was only in the field of actual combat that the Mozambican people were at first able to cast aside their feeling of inferiority. In battle, they shed their blinkers. Every Portuguese, killed, wounded or captured in battle had the effect of blowing sky high the myth of the invincibility of the Portuguese, or his superiority. They found the Portuguese were simply human beings like themselves who cried out in pain from wounds as much as they did. And amongst the Portuguese they found men who were timid and cowardly. But they also found that there were Portuguese who surrendered not because of cowardice, but because they believed that the cause that Salazar and Caetano stood for was the wrong cause, and that Frelimo was fighting a just war. Thus in a period of a few years of actual combat, the Mozambican people were able to discard the slave mentality which the colonizers through their agents had tried to inculcate. They no longer believed the myth of racial superiority and inferiority.

Those Portuguese who had deserted to Frelimo, though few in number, were more important to Mondlane than even a company of enemy soldiers captured or killed. In war, it is not only military strength that is important. It is equally important, if not more important to win the battle of the mind. If Frelimo could convince a section of the enemy soldiers that theirs was a just war and against oppression and not against race, then half the battle was won. In Indo-China, the People's Liberation forces have been able to undermine the enemy's morale in this way with great success.

Mondlane appreciated this aspect of the struggle. Just as there was no place in his mental makeup for tribalism, so too with racialism. His education, his contact with people of all races, of all colours and creeds was such as to make him cut across artificial divisions that separated human beings. He looked at human beings as they should be looked at, namely in terms of what contribution to humanity generally and to the Mozambican revolution in particular they were making.

But not all members of Frelimo regarded the struggle in the same way as Mondlane. In fact he was soon to encounter racialism in reverse. There were a few among the top leadership who believed that all Portuguese were oppressors and exploiters. Thus, what was essentially a war between the oppressor and oppressed, between colonial masters and colonial slaves, was turned into a racial war between white and black. This went against the grain with Mondlane, who had fought white racialism all his life and therefore would have no truck with black racialism. He also understood the logic of where such an outlook would lead. The monster of racialism if unchecked could wreck what he and his colleagues had built up. Today it could be against the Portuguese, tomorrow it would be against other white men. The following day it could be against the mulattoes and other minority groups. Such thinking would also degenerate into inter-tribal fights. Frelimo in establishing a national Front, embraced not only all the classes but also all the tribes and minority groups. Racialism if unchecked would tend to undermine the national Front, and this could only benefit the Portuguese.

The racialism in reverse campaign was conducted underground. At that time Mondlane did not suspect that this was being used as a weapon to undermine his position as President because his wife was an American. However, he raised the issue on a number of occasions to draw out those who stood for such ideas. But none would come out openly and defend black racialism publicly. At the Second Congress of Frelimo, Mondlane was able to get the endorsement of the Congress on the resolution regarding the question of prisoners-of-war. After stating that the prisoner-of-war should be well treated, the resolution stated: 'We may also use prisoners as hostages to be exchanged for our comrades who may be in the Portuguese colonial prisons. In this way, we would be showing to the world that we are fighting against Portuguese colonialism and not against the Portuguese people; we would be breaking the fighting morale of the enemy's army, and encouraging its soldiers' desertions. The Second Congress decides, therefore, that Frelimo should continue to apply the policy of clemency with regard to captured enemy soldiers.'[38]

As a result, not only was Mondlane able to use the most advanced ideas as regards the humane treatment of prisoners-of-war, but he was also able to axe away the foundations of the racialists, who would if they had their way have killed every Portuguese who fell into their hands.

I I

Portugal's counter-attack; The Cabora Bassa Dam

WITHIN two years of launching the armed struggle, it became quite clear to Portugal that Frelimo guerrillas, like the Guinea Bissau, Angolan and Mozambican freedom fighters were there to stay, and that the offensives to liquidate them had failed. Portugal was engaged in a protracted struggle which tied down at least 200,000 of her troops, using the best materials which NATO could supply. This also meant that over half her budget, which totalled over £150 million, was spent on defence. This had a disastrous effect on her own internal development, and small wonder Portugal remains the poorest country in Europe with the lowest per capita income.

The representatives of the national liberation movements

in all three Portuguese colonial territories in Africa have maintained that Portugal would not have been able to afford to sustain such a drain on her resources were it not that she has been aided and abetted by the NATO powers. This is specially the case with the supply of arms, for Portugal has no armament factories of her own. The NATO powers believed that Portugal would achieve a quick victory over the 'rebels'. But as in the case of Angola, the liberation struggle which took the road of armed revolt was already ten years old by 1971. The imperialist powers seeing no immediate profit for themselves have now been given a stake in Portugal's projected Cabora Bassa Dam.

The dam is to be constructed on the Zambezi River in the Tete province about one hundred and fifty miles from the Zambian border. Its significance lies in the fact that if built it would be the largest dam in Africa, costing over £125 million sterling. Its total capacity would be 3.6 million kws per year, and its operating costs would be 0.35 cents per Kw, making it one of the cheapest in the world.

However, Salazar who launched this scheme knew this would never have left the blue print stage were it not that there was a crisis in South Africa as regards electricity. South Africa lacks large navigable rivers. Few have water all the year round. Electricity from existing sources has reached a saturation point. The phenomenal industrial advance, largely due to the exploitation of cheap labour from the gold mines, gave it surplus capital to start on industrial ventures. By 1968, when the Cabora Bassa Scheme was officially mooted, South Africa was already consuming 57% of the total electricity consumption for the whole continent. If there was to be any further industrial development, particularly around the Witwatersrand industrial complex it became imperative for this problem to be solved. The planners had looked around and found in the Ox bow Scheme of Lesotho a reasonable possibility. But this could only be a temporary stop gap for within another ten years it would soon be faced with another crisis. It was Dr Van Eck, the boss of the ISCOR, the steel complex in the Transvaal who now decided that it would be good for South Africa's

1 Samora Moises Machel

4   *Mondlane and Machel*

7 *Janet Mondlane*

8   *Chude Mondlane*

interests to strengthen further the economic bonds with Portugal, and thus supported the idea of the construction of the Cabora Bassa. The dam would also make all sorts of mineral and industrial development possible in Mozambique and with the extra one million white settlers would strengthen Portugal's presence in the country, and imperialism in southern Africa.

The attitude of the Western powers was that they would help in the construction, for a £125 million project was not to be scoffed at. Such opportunities don't come every day. They also wanted to see Portuguese power in Mozambique strengthened. However, they demanded security. They wanted to be sure that not only would there be economic, but also military backing apart from Portugal. This meant South African involvement. They indicated that they were not prepared to go it alone. The tenders which were called for by Salazar each consisted therefore of a consortia of firms. Three such consortia submitted tenders, and in each of them there was a South African firm. After much delay, the contract was finally awarded to the Zambesi Consortium. This consisted of monopolies from four countries. They were:

West Germany: Siemens, Telefunken, Brown Boveri, Hotchief and J. M. Voith.
France: Alsthom, C.C.I. Cogolex and C.C.G.E.
Sweden: ASEA.
South Africa: L.T.A. and Vecor.

Behind all this may be seen the hand of Oppenheimer, concealed behind the comparatively unknown construction Company the L.T.A., which is a subsidiary of the giant multi-national Anglo American Corporation with headquarters in South Africa. This Company got over 35% of the engineering contract. Harry Oppenheimer is on the Board of Directors of Barclays Bank as well as on the Banque de Paris. His Anglo American Corporation has vast liquid financial resources. For the 51% take over by the Zambian government of his shares in the copper mines he received over £50 million.

The fact that Portugal was only committed to putting up

20% of the total cost shows both its economic weakness, and the extent of support from South Africa and Western nations. Major firms from Italy, Sweden, Britain, and now the U.S.A. have since dropped out of the project. Britain's action has been characteristically hypocritical. While British companies have withdrawn from the actual project British factories are being set up in Mozambique which would not have been feasible without Cabora Bassa. Nevertheless, these withdrawals do weaken the chances of the dam being built.

Mondlane realized the danger to the Mozambican struggle which the Cabora Bassa posed. South Africa was not only involved in the construction and financing, but it also cornered 80% of the total supply. The power would be A/C current by pylons running from the site to the Witwatersrand, a distance of over 1,000 miles. The decision to build the dam brought the South African troops right into Mozambique although they denied this. They were stationed at the Cabora Bassa site. What the South Africans did admit was that they were sending 100 'male nurses' to help in the fight 'against Communism'. So behind political reasons there were hard economic considerations.

Similarly, although the French and West German monopolies tendered, the governments were also directly involved. Thus, in the case of the latter, the firms were to be given a loan through the government controlled Reconstruction Loan Corporation of a 50 million dollar credit to be paid after 1975 when the dam is expected to be completed.

Frelimo decided that every effort should be made to block the construction of the dam. Logistically it would not have been feasible to launch this campaign from the bases of Cabo Delgado and Niassa. Hence a new front had to be opened. After the Second Congress, Mondlane was able to announce that Frelimo had moved from the phase of ambushes, and was concentrating in attacking the enemy garrison posts, and in isolating the towns in which he was hiding. A new Front was established in the Tete province. Later Frelimo raised the slogan: 'Cabora Bassa Delenda Est' – Cabora Bassa must be destroyed.

African states as a whole, with the exception of Zambia and Tanzania, have not appreciated sufficiently the danger that the Cabora Bassa poses to the whole of Africa. Once South Africa is assured of this vital electric supply it would be able to maintain its industrial leadership of the whole continent, and in that way dominate Africa. Secondly, Portugal plans to plant one million settlers there. Who will these be, but firstly the demobilized soldiers and their families. They will be bent on aggression and grab more and more territory from neighbouring African states. This would mean that Africa could be faced with another phase of white colonization.

Tanzania has provided Frelimo with a reliable base area and it is therefore not surprising the greatest success has been recorded in those provinces which adjoin this territory. And in unfolding People's War, it is from the liberated areas that the waves begin to flow onwards.

The new Front involved hazardous communication lines, and many doubted the feasibility of the venture. Was it tactically wise to scatter forces when they should be able to concentrate as well as to consolidate? Would they be able to sustain such a Front? However, some of the logistical problems seemed to have been solved when the Portuguese began to launch savage raids on Zambian villages on the Mozambican border near the site of the Cabora Bassa Dam. The Portuguese believed that Frelimo had begun to operate from the Zambian side of the border and that Zambia was in fact performing the same function as Tanzania, of providing it with a rear.

How effective has the Front been? Two years after the struggle began in this area the head of the sabotage section and also a member of the Frelimo Central Committee was interviewed. These are the questions and answers:

'Question: Comrade, can you tell us in a general way how our struggle in the Tete province is developing?

Answer: Our struggle here started two years ago, but we have been able to inflict hard blows on the enemy, forcing them to abandon many of their fortified positions. We can

83

say that the whole part north of the Zambesi River is affected by the war. The Portuguese built many fortified posts to prevent our guerrillas from crossing. We are already on the other side ... one post, Demeciano, was attacked three times by our forces, and the enemy left in a hurry. They had no time to burn their houses; our forces took away the corrugated iron roofs which are now being used by our people. South of the Zambesi we are not engaged in military operations, only clandestine political work.[39] Frelimo forces have since crossed the river, and the Portuguese now admit guerrilla activities south of the Zambesi.

COREMO (Revolutionary Committee of Mozambique), the other nationalist organization based in Lusaka, has also been operating in the Tete District. Mondlane states that it is one of the groups that started military action inside Mozambique in 1965. Although he believed that they were crushed immediately, it appears that they are very much alive and active. They have had stiffer odds to face than Frelimo in that they have not been recognized by the OAU, but they are still able to conduct an armed struggle. Mondlane said that divisive conduct could be due to individual differences, neurosis, personal ambitions and that there could be real ideological differences. But these must be looked at against the background of what unites these organizations. Firstly, Coremo stands for independence from Portugal. It believes in armed struggle through the tactics of guerrilla warfare, with the main direction of activity in the countryside. Coremo believes in an anti-imperialist struggle, and on the vital issue of the Cabora Bassa Dam agrees with Frelimo that it must be destroyed. It must be stated within the rank and file of both Frelimo and Coremo there is tacit understanding.

While African leaders have no desire to interfere in the internal affairs of national liberation movements, yet they have been urging organizations operating in a single country to unite. Kwame Nkrumah, whenever it was possible, has always urged different groups to come together. Now there is a clear need for Frelimo to think of a united Front with

Coremo, particularly since both are committed to the destruction of the Cabora Bassa Dam. Such a Front would not necessitate either Frelimo or Coremo giving up their identity. They could retain it with the right of freedom of action and even of criticism of the other. All this is possible under a united Front. A united Front conceived with the proper spirit would provide a lead to other nationalist organizations, for it would be a Front of those who are actively involved in the struggle. A united Front would make it easier for genuine revolutionary elements to get rid of any bogus membership and to purge the Party. Such a united Front could be a great blow to the enemy, and it would hearten the people and encourage them to redouble their efforts.

I2

The role of women in the Mozambican revolution

THE advent of private property, a feature of civilization, not only split society between two hostile and irreconcilable classes, but also saw the rise of the patriarchal household where the paterfamilias was given the power of life and death over his wife and children. The woman in this society lost her position of equality which she enjoyed in earlier communal society. From an elevated and honourable position, the woman now became degraded and debased. She was treated like a chattel, and was in fact regarded as another piece of private property. In a polygamous household, a characteristic feature of certain African societies, her position further deteriorated. Not only was the relationship of equality riddled through and through both economically and socially, but on the plane of the most basic, human and delicate level of sexual relationships, man and woman here appeared as unequals.

But nowhere did the position of women sink to such a low, degrading and humiliating level as under colonial domination. Here she suffered oppression and exploitation. Not only did the women suffer national oppression and class exploitation like the men, but she also suffered oppression and even exploitation because of her sex. Janet Mondlane, wife and companion of Eduardo Mondlane till his death, has told of the heavy hand of oppression and cruelty as experienced by the Mozambican women. In an address to the World Congress of Women held in Helsinki in June, 1969,* she describes the plight of the women of Mozambique in these words: 'To be brutally frank, she is often more despised than a barnyard animal and is considered only useful as a producer of children . . . she is a slave of her husband. Much of the labour in the fields is her responsibility to first clear the bush, then to tend the crops under the burning sun, with hunger in her body.'[40] And on the havoc that the migratory system of labour as well as of forced labour which wrenched her husband, brother or son away from home, thus forcing her to look after the children she says: 'It is a common sight to see women walking along the roads, selling wood, food or some small produce to support the children. And sometimes she has no alternative but to sell her own body as well. . . . A Portuguese colonialist sees the African woman as an instrument to satisfy his personal interest. A woman is issued an official document to legitimize her status of prostitution.'[41]

Mondlane was way ahead of many African leaders in his championing the cause of women. He was moved by the degradation of womanhood caused by centuries of oppression. It appalled him that women should be reduced to such a low level as to be treated no differently than beasts. His relationship with Janet, a fellow student whom he met while she was still at secondary school and whom he subsequently married, could not have been but on the basis of equality. And it was this concept of equality that he tried to bring to the Mozambican people. He did much to uplift them and endow them with a dignity which was their due. The true test of any revolutionary is whether he is prepared to take up the cudgels on behalf of the oppressed and exploited wherever they may be, or whoever they may be. His sensitivity to this issue made him agree with the forthright

* Appendix Three

criticim of Rene Dumont who said that the African woman has suffered a type of economic exploitation, having had to bear the brunt of labour to support the whole society. In some instances she has suffered social restrictions and has been denied a place of influence in the family and larger community.

Just as he fought tribalism and racialism, Mondlane also struggled against practices based on sexual discrimination. He encouraged women to join the army, which improved their position. Of this he says: 'By accepting women into its ranks, it has revolutionized their social position. Women now play a very active part in running popular militias, and there are also many guerrilla units composed of women. Through the army, women have started to take responsibility in many areas; they have learned to stand up and speak at public meetings, to take an active part in politics. ... The sight of armed women who get up and talk in front of large audiences caused great amazement, even incredulity.'[42]

One of the reasons why he was able to recruit large numbers of women into the ranks of Frelimo was that he was prepared to listen to them. He quotes an example when, 'I addressed a meeting in Mozambique early in 1968 and the people began asking questions, a woman in one of the women's units got up and complained that women were not being trained as officers, so that all the officers were men.' And Mondlane instead of rationalizing said quite honestly: 'Nobody thought of making women officers.'[43] As a direct consequence of this, a decision was taken that in future women would be able to become officers when they had suitable qualifications and experience.

The women themselves have expressed gratitude for what the Revolution has done for them and what it means to them now. Frelimo has given them a voice as well as an honourable role to play, not only in production, but also in the actual struggle. According to one of the militants, the Mozambican woman joins the militias which protect the people and the fields. She carries weapons, and when necessary fights in combat units.

One woman leader which the Mozambican revolution

produced was Josina Abiathar Muthemba. This is what she had to say: 'Before the struggle, even in our society women had an inferior position. Today in Frelimo, the Mozambican woman has a voice and an important role to play; she can express her opinions; she is free to say what she likes. She has the same rights and duties as any militant, because she is Mozambican, because in our Party there is no discrimination based on sex.'[44]

The Mozambican Revolution released the creative energies of Josina Muthemba which could not be expressed in the old society. She rose rapidly in Frelimo, for it needed her talents. But like Mondlane she did not live to see the end of the Revolution, for at the age of 25 she died in Dar es Salaam, just two years after the death of her first President. But the Josinas in their thousands, who have been freed by the Revolution, live to carry on the struggle.

Through the Mozambican Revolution, the women are coming back into their own. It is to Mondlane that credit should go in setting in motion the process of liberation for women who occupied the lowest rung in African society. In giving them a vision of a new life he was able to release a vital force of creative energy. In doing so he was beginning to transform step by step the Mozambican struggle for liberation into a People's War in which everyone, man, woman and child is involved.

13

Poetry in the Mozambican revolution

THE pre-revolutionary era of Mozambique produced some of the most sensitive and passionate poetry known to Africa. Beginning with the poetry of doubt about the new order, including its new religion, Christianity, it moved to a plane of rebellion at the harsh and ruthless exploitation of the people. This became one of the most important tributaries that has fed the poetry of the present Mozambican Revolution. Poetry of the people, that is from the toilers and tillers has been embodied in folklore, song and dance. In the main it was oral. But together with the other forms of art, namely sculpture and carving, it shows the people's resentment, anger and hostility at the new values imposed on them under the guise of Western Christian civilization. Mondlane relates how the Makonde carvings, when they broke through the commercialism which sometimes affected them, showed remarkable insight and perception. In these carvings the artist indicts and condemns the new values. The madonna is given a demon to hold instead of the child Christ; the priest is represented with the feet of a wild animal, and the pieta is shown as a mother raising a spear over the body of her dead son.

The same spirit is also shown in the poetry of the people. Thus the Chope say:

> We are still angry; it is always the same,
> The oldest daughters must always pay the tax. . . .

and in exposing a government stooge they sang:

> For the man they have appointed is a son of nobody,
> The Chope have lost the right to own their land.

Frelimo poets and militants have seen the need to put into writing the folklore of the people, their tales and songs about events and everyday life. A move is being made to salvage this portion of their heritage before it is lost to posterity.

The written poetry before the revolution came from the mulattoes and the assimmiladoes, that is the section of the Mozambican population which had managed to escape the rigours of toil and labour in the plantations, mines, factories and docks. Once they had acquired the art of reading, a whole new world lay before them. But these intellectuals' horizons were widening at a time when liberal democracy had given way to Salazar's fascist dictatorship. This tyrant banned all political organization and purged the universities of not only the radical elements but also the liberals. Hundreds of those workers accused of being communists were sent to the gallows or allowed to rot and die in the prisons which were overflowing with inmates who opposed his dictatorship. Conformity in thought was the rule, and was carried out with zeal and fanaticism. To show any doubt on any political policies was enough to bring the dreaded security police knocking at one's doors in the middle of the night. In Salazar's colonies it was even worse. Innocent economic organizations like the cooperatives and trade unions were kept under strict surveillance and the dreaded PIDE shadows appeared everywhere. Under such an atmosphere, it was understandable that there could be no political activity let alone any political organizations. Newspapers which expressed political views just folded up. Therefore the torment of the intellectual, his anguish, frustration, outraged feelings, shock and rebellion expressed itself in poetry.

In the early decades of the twentieth century, cries of self-pity were isolated. The earliest poet of note was Rui de Noronha (1909–1943). He had accepted the new Christian religion as well as its God in the hope that this would lead to the salvation he was seeking. But in his 'Supplica', he realizes that this was leading him to a dead end. He questions, and he does so in this way:

> Where are you, who are you O powerful God,
> Who I cannot know, nor understand?

He later accuses for:

> If God is just, why do I know only evil and
> injustice?

His own inner anguish and restless longing, his growing disillusionment with the new world springing from Portuguese colonization made him look keenly at the misery and suffering all around him:

> O negroes, how painful is it to live
> a whole life under the load of others
> and in old age the bread of charity.

A poet sometimes is like a mirror. He reflects distortions, and for that he is assailed. But at times he is just reflecting reality and not something from his own imagination. If Noronha's poetry is one of doubt, it reflected the political consciousness of the times. Few intellectuals had worked out analytically the nature of oppression, examined its various aspects and then on the basis of that arrived at a solution. That was to come later. But in his 'Surge et Ambula', he caught the new breeze that was blowing throughout Africa for he wrote:

Wake up, your sleep is deeper than the earth
Listen to the voices of progress, that other Nazarene,
Who holds out his hand and says, 'Africa – get up and Go.'

The later poets wrote about the ruthless exploitation and suppression of the Mozambicans, of their wasted youth, frustrated hopes and anguished cries. At this time the ideas of equality and freedom for the submerged masses of Africa had come to the fore. The poets had drunk from the deep wells of knowledge. They had come into contact with revolutionary ideas some of which they made their own. We see this evolution in the writings of Noémia de Sousa, one of the representatives of the Craveirinha group.

As mentioned earlier, over 100,000 Mozambicans were compelled to work annually in the South African mines. This wrecked the internal equilibrium of the economy and stunted its growth. The family system was destroyed and the position of the mine worker, who produced the wealth for the rulers of South Africa and the parasites overseas, was abject and miserable. His poverty and his exploitation excited the passions of many poets of this generation. Thus Noémia de Sousa unfolds in her 'Magaiça', the tragedy of a blighted and wasted youth:

Bemused Magaiça lit the lamp
to look for lost illusions,
his youth, his health which stayed behind
deep in the mines of Johannesburg.

In her poem, 'Let My People go', we see how she is inspired by the freedom struggles elsewhere, although she cannot see any way out in Mozambique:

Voices from America, stir my soul and nerves,
And Robeson and Marion sing for me,
Let my People Go – Oh let my People Go,
they say;

I open my eyes and cannot sleep,
Andersen and Paul sing for me,
And they are not the soft voices of a lullaby,
Let my people Go.

The rise of the oppressed masses in Mozambique following the heroic strike of the African mine workers in South Africa in 1946, had its ripples in Mozambique where a series of strikes broke out, led by the dockworkers. These spread to the plantations and shook the whole fabric of Portuguese rule. Vengeance was harsh, cruel and pitiless. Hundreds were arrested and deported. One of those to suffer was João, Noémia's companion and she wrote:

But what matter?
They have stolen João from us
but João is us all
Because of that João hasn't left us . . .
For João is us all, we are a multitude
and the multitude
Who can carry off a multitude and lock it in a cage?

From seeing herself as an individual, there grows in her a social awareness that she is part of the new nation that is being born out of suffering and pain:

If you want to know who I am . . .
Ah, she is who I am,
empty eye sockets, despairing of possessing life,
a mouth slashed with wounds of anguish . . .
body tattooed with visible and invisible scars
by the hard whips of slavery . . .

And ask me nothing more,
if you really wish to know me,

for I am no more than a shell of fish,
in which the revolt of Africa congealed
its cry swollen with hope . . .

Poetry of doubt has given way to rebellion, sometimes
personal, often political and social. Craveirinha, writing with
all the strength and force at his command, attacks the savage
system of exploitation in the mines in his famous poem
'Grito Negro' – Black Cry.

I am coal!
You tear me brutally from the ground
and make of me your mine, boss

I am coal
and you burn me, boss
to serve you forever as your driving force
but not forever, boss
I am coal
and must burn
and consume everything in the heat of my combustion

I am coal
and must burn, exploited
burn alive like tar, my brother
until no more your mine, boss

I am coal
and must burn
and consume everything in the heat of my combustion

Yes, boss
I will be your coal!

Not forever boss – with these words the poet was able to
capture the new mood and ferment amongst the new generation of toilers. With his sensitive 'antennae', he could sense
the change that was taking place amongst the toilers. Here

93

he spoke specifically of the mine worker, but by catching the general mood, he was letting sparks fly. In his way the poet was proclaiming the death of the old order and heralding the birth of the new.

Mondlane, himself an intellectual, but who had broken loose, understood only too well how the poets, once properly orientated could play an important part in the unfolding Mozambican revolution. If he was aware of their potentialities, he also knew only too well their limitations, the chief one being that they were divorced from the masses. It has been said quite correctly that until the 19th century the philosophers were content to interpret the world. Since that did not involve any social action by anybody, there was a great deal of quibbling about words. But then a new school arose which said that philosophy should aim at interpreting the world in order to change it. What this meant was that the philosopher had to enter the broad stream of political struggle. With poetry too it was the same. The radical poets and novelists in the West have written about the rot and decadence that has set in, in Western society. With a keen eye they have delineated the idleness, corruption and parasitism of the upper classes, and the degradation and dehumanization of the toilers and tillers. They also wrote with fire and enthusiasm of the sporadic and protracted revolt of the workers and peasants. But when it came to the question of completely identifying themselves with the masses, they have been found wanting.

It was the same with the bulk of the pre-revolutionary poets and writers. They had sensed the new mood of revolt amongst the people. But when it came to committing themselves to the organization that was fighting for the new order of society which they themselves had longed for, not only for themselves but also the people about whom they had written, they were found to be wanting. Mondlane made great efforts to persuade them to join Frelimo, for only in the struggle would their poetry assume the grandeur and splendour which characterize great works of art. He himself did not believe he was wholly successful for he says: 'Few of Craveirinha's group succeeded in escaping from their isolation and bridging the gap between theory and practice. Noémia de Sousa left Mozambique, has stopped writing poetry, and now lives in Paris ... only Marcelino dos Santos, after a long period of exile in Europe, joined the liberation movement, and since then his poetry has changed and developed under the impetus of the armed struggle.'[45] It is doubtful if his strictures on the poets and artists are completely justified. Some of them could not join because they were in jail, while others remaining in Mozambique were closely watched. Further, an intellectual has to be treated with patience. It takes him longer to break with bourgeois society than the worker and peasant. Therefore he should be pursued and brought back to the Revolution even if it takes a matter of years.

If only a few joined the revolutionary stream, the work of these poets was not in vain. They had sowed the seeds for a new generation of intellectuals who inspired by their writings had the youth and idealism to push ahead to their rightful home – Frelimo. From the very start they were involved in the revolutionary struggle and knew of no other life but that. Poetry was transformed and so was its function. Poetry by a small group of intellectuals for an equally small group that characterized pre-revolutionary poetry becomes poetry for the people, a vital instrument in the struggle for liberation.

Mondlane did not deal extensively with the poetry of the Revolution. But he knew that in the context of the armed struggle, a new literary tradition was taking place giving it a rich, healthy hue. The militants began to produce their own monthly magazine aptly called *25 de Septembero* and here the young political thinkers, artists and poets gave vent to their inner thoughts and feelings. If theirs was one of heightened sensitivity, with strong passionate feelings, it was because the lives they lived were unusual. There were heroic deeds by their comrades, foul and senseless killings by the oppressors, joy in victory, sadness and grief at the passing away of a comrade. What they wrote about is what they experienced themselves. Mondlane however was able to see the significance of the new trend in Mozambican poetry for as he said, 'When Noémia, Craveirinha and dos Santos were

writing their eloquent denunciation of Portuguese colonialism, they were not read by the people they were writing
about. Now the work of a good poet in Frelimo will be read
in the camps by the militants, by the people drawn from the
exploited masses, who in the past were simply the subjects of
poems by poets they had never heard of ... the gap between
the intellectual and the people is closing.'[46]

One feature of the new poetry he was able to discern was
the medium by which it was being conveyed to the people.
Western art including its literature in its period of decline
had degenerated into a state where to hide the poverty of its
content, it adorned itself with ornamental and flowery
phrases which had meaning only to a few. Detached from
the people, these artists have made no attempts to reach the
people. Now here in the new revolutionary poetry a conscious attempt was made to adopt a simple style which could
be understood by the people. Thus in Rebelo's poem where
dreams of revolt become a reality he wants to:

> forge simple words
> that even children can understand,
> words which will enter every house,
> like the wind,
> and fall like red hot embers,
> on our peoples souls,
> (for) in our land, bullets are beginning to flower.

Mondlane was aware that an attempt was being made to
present a systematic account of the growth of the poetry of
the Mozambican Revolution. A number of young poets with
talent had sprung up like Gustave Milton, Bebe, Moguimo,
Mario Sive, Malido, Savio, Mchika, Dick Vovotti and
Cosme. The writings of these as well as the older ones of
Santos, Rebelo and Guebuza appeared in an excellent analysis of the development of Mozambican poetry in the
March/April issue 1969 of the 'Mozambican Revolution.'
The January/February issue of the same year carried an
account of the earlier poets. The poetry is analysed against
the social milieu and the prevailing political climate in each
phase. The searching, the frustration, the doubt of Noronha

are delineated gently but without sentiment, while the anguish, cries and rebellion of Noémia de Sousa is shown with all the sympathy that one has for the Hamlets of life. It shows how she came to the brink of the Revolution in her poetry, but in life was never able to cross the Rubicon. Its other merit lies in the presentation to the world at large of the new generation of writers, showing talent and promise, who are drawing all the time sustenance from the soil of the Revolution for it is poetry born out of action and the necessities of the present.

The hero, and there could be no other in the prevailing climate, is the guerrilla, who has given to Frelimo his most precious possession, his life, for the sake of the Revolution. This is how the poet Cosme sees him in his 'O Guerrilheiro'

> There he comes, armed and fierce,
> there comes a man who brings freedom,
> ragged and dirty, but with an iron heart,
> the guerrilla smiles and sings,
>
> He has no house, little food and clothes,
> he lives through suffering all,
> the torrential rain beats against him,
> the bitter cold bites harshly,
> still he smiles and sings,
>
> I bring peace and freedom,
> With this weapon in my hand,
> I'll drive out Salazar and his troops.

The poetry reaches universality in the selection of its themes. Eduardo Tome is slain in battle and his companion Omar Juma writes about this event. His poem could have been written in the deserts of Palestine by the fedayeen or by the liberation forces in Indo China. He writes what could be the epitaph for his departed comrade:

> In the last moment of your life you said,
> Dear Comrade, take my gun,

97

I can no longer fight,
too soon was I hit by the enemy's bullet
quickly take my gun and carry on. . . .

I believe in you, Hero,
man with a heart of steel,
I will follow your example,
with all my strength and dedication,
for consolation as a friend
and joy as a hero!

The poet in Mozambique is not cut off from the vital activities of life, nor from the people. He is a Man whose development is rounded. He is a soldier, producer, administrator as well as a poet and artist. He sees himself not as an individual but part of a wider social community. Joys, sorrows and action is shared collectively. Thus Armando Guebuza writes:

Your anguish,
joined with mine,
will rise to strangle oppression,
together with mine
speak of revolt. . . .

Your blood together with mine,
will water the seeds of victory.

Bebe in 1967 takes the theme of a poem written in 1953 by Marcelino dos Santos. He starts on the same note and then strikes out on his own individual path. This is a brilliant example of detournement. This more than any other shows the growth of the Mozambican revolutionary poetry, while at the same time revealing its origin. It also highlights the distance the Revolution has travelled and the confidence it has given its participants.

Santos: 1953.

No
seek me not
in places where I don't exist.

I live
hunched over the earth
following the path cut by the whip
on my naked back

I live in the harbours,
feeding the furnaces,
driving the machines,
along the paths of men

I live
in the body of my mother,
selling her strength in
the market place. . . .

I live
lost in the streets
of a civilization
that crushes me with hatred
and without pity.

And if it is my voice that is heard,
if it is I who still sing,
It is because I cannot die,
But only the moon hears my anguish. . . .

I am there in America also,
Yes, I am
. . .
if I am here,
vibrantly alive
in the voice of Robeson and Hughes
of Cesaire and Guillen
Godido and Black Boy Reborn . . .

If I am here, and solid incarnation
the conscious
of men,
who composed the poems,
of life and death,

of the end of night,
and the coming of the day.

Bebe: 1967.

No
seek me not
I am not lost

I live,
strong and determined,
following the path
cut by Freedom
through fangs and claws of oppression

I live,
in my people
firing my guns and bazookas
  along the road to peace.

I live,
in the body of my mother earth,
Using the strength that is mine. . . .

I live,
one with the masses,
with a protection that shelters me,
with hatred for the enemy,
complete and unreserved.

And if it is my shots which are heard,
and I who still fight on,
it is because I shall never retreat,
never, never, never
until my people prevail

I am here in Mozambique also,
yes I am,
if I am here vibrantly alive,
in the voice of the people and of heroes,
Gungunghana and Maguiguana,
Warriors of Africa reborn

If I am here,
alert,
strong,
day, night,
until victory,
I am here.

One of the reasons for the flowering of Mozambican poetry
has been the ability of the poets to synthesize the old with
the new. The Mozambican revolutionaries analysed Western
culture and found it decadent. They fought the tendency
prevalent in some African countries to inflict on the young
nation, the cynicism and sickness of the West. On the other
hand they saw that culture, past or present, is part of man's
heritage. In the literary field as in the political, military and
socio-economic fields they selected the good and rejected the
bad. The revolutionary ideas from the West, political or literary, its spirit of scientific analysis and methods, its experiences of the oppressed and exploited they took and made
their own. They used the same standard when it came to the
selection from their own past. They selected what was good
in the past and which colonialism had tried to destroy.

Just as there could be no return to tribal society, so too
there can be no return to tribal culture and reactionary institutions like polygamy which degraded womanhood to the
level of slaves. Poetry embodying the myths and super-
stitions of the tribal era is valuable only from a historical
point of view and as a standard to show the progress the
people in their Revolution have made. It has become a practice by certain elements of the indigenous bourgeoisie, insti-
gated by imperialism, to revive in the past culture those
traditions and practices which have become obsolete. The
aim is to cut Africans off from the main stream of historical
development. That is what Verwoerd, the South African
Prime Minister tried to do. He wanted the African to go
back to the days of tribalism, with archaic tribal practices
and rituals. In this way, he hoped to ensure white domination for another three hundred years.

Mozambican poetry, because it has taken the best from

the present and its own past, and because the artist is now linked with the broad stream of life, is showing a new vigour and vitality. Being young, the poetry of the Revolution is also optimistic, for 'poems are one expression of the amount of creative energy unchained by the Revolution, which does not necessarily and always go into actions, thoughts, and feelings. These poems are part of a larger reality. The proof is that poetry is no longer a specialization. There is no poet left, because everybody is a poet. Tomorrow there will be no master left because everybody will be the master of himself.'[47]

Finally, the following lines written by Mondlane's successor, Samora Moises Machel, in July 1971, in memory of Josina, a leading Frelimo woman militant, who died tragically while in her early twenties:

Josina, you are not dead

Josina you are not dead because we have assumed your responsibilities and they live in us.

You have not died for the causes you championed were inherited by us in their entirety.

You are gone from us, but the weapon and rucksack that you left, your tools of work, are part of my burden.

The blood you shed is but a small drop in the flood we have already given and still have to give.

The earth must be nourished and the more fertile it is the better do its trees flourish, the bigger are the shadows they cast, the sweeter are their fruits.

Out of your memory I will fashion a hoe to turn the sod enriched by your sacrifice. . . . And new fruits will grow.

The Revolution renews itself from its best and most beloved children.

This is the meaning of your sacrifice: it will be a living example to be followed.

My joy is that as patriot and woman you died doubly free in this time when the new power and the new woman are emerging.

In your last moments you apologized to the doctors for not being able to help them.

The manner in which you accepted the sacrifice is an inexhaustible source of inspiration and courage.

When a comrade so completely assumes the new values he wins our hearts, becomes our banner.

Thus more than wife, you were to me sister, friend and comrade-in-arms.

How can we mourn a comrade but by holding the fallen gun and continuing the combat.

My tears flow from the same source that gave birth to our love, our will and our revolutionary life.

Thus these tears are both a token and a vow of combat.

The flowers which fall from the tree are to prepare the land for new and more beautiful flowers to bloom in the next season.

Your life continues in those who continue the Revolution.

14

The Second Congress of Frelimo

THE growth of Frelimo as a result of the launching of the armed struggle brought with it a train of problems which needed discussion and clarification, so that the people engaged in the struggle would know just where Frelimo stood on a number of crucial issues. Apart from the question of how to govern the liberated zones, there were a whole range of questions on social affairs as well as armed struggle needing clarification.

For some time, particularly after late 1967, there were suggestions that another Congress of Frelimo should be convened. It is true there were certain elements who had begun to question Mondlane's leadership and there were also a few ugly incidents in Dar es Salaam. But that was not the main reason which impelled Mondlane to call a conference. He gave an explanation himself when he said that the need for a conference had been stressed by several missions of the Central Committee which had been visiting the liberated areas. He felt himself the time was ripe, for there were problems of a political and social nature which needed discussion. He pinpointed some of these as the working relationship between civilian and military administration in liberated areas; ways to increase agricultural production; the role of cooperatives; commerce, and cottage industries. However, what was not stated explicitly, but was clear to impartial observers, was that by 1968 the composition of the Central Committee no longer corresponded to reality. Some of the older members of the Central Committee had dropped by the wayside. Others could not keep pace with the growth of the armed struggle. On the other hand, the Revolution had thrown up a new, younger leadership which had already distinguished itself, not only as regards its political commitment, but also in the military field. They already had support amongst the people and Frelimo militants and freedom fighters but were not on the Central Committee.

The first Congress had been held in Dar es Salaam. A clear indication of the strides which Frelimo had made was that Mondlane was able to announce publicly that the Second Congress would be held somewhere inside Mozambique. He even stated the month of September, although in fact it was held in July 1968. That it was held in one of the liberated areas nailed the lie that Portugal controlled the whole of Mozambique and that Frelimo just consisted of roving bands without any fixed base. Some might doubt Mondlane's wisdom in announcing publicly not only the holding of the Congress but also the time. But it showed Mondlane's confidence in the strength of Frelimo that he dared the Portuguese to stop them.

Just what the launching of the armed struggle involving the whole population had done to the movement for national liberation could be seen by the attendance at the Congress. Mondlane who was to preside over the Congress said that the accomplishment of Frelimo's political organizations was shown by the presence of delegates from all over

Mozambique, even from the far south. There for the first time in this history, Mozambicans from all over the territory were gathered to discuss together the problems of the whole nation and take decisions which would affect the whole future. Delegates were from different tribes and religious groups and there were women participating as well as men. This was an indication of the distance Frelimo had travelled in the last four years.

The Congress proceedings did not differ materially from those of other national movements engaged in armed struggle. Delegates from each region as well as heads of departments presented reports over work done in the past few years. There were discussions and debates on each of these and delegates were at liberty to ask questions and to make criticisms.

After clarification by the leadership of a number of questions on matters of policy a number of resolutions were drafted and presented for approval by Congress. They gave a clear indication of the policy and aims of Frelimo for the next four years. The resolutions dealt with armed struggle, administration of liberated zones, national reconstruction, social affairs and foreign policy.

The most significant resolution was undoubtedly the one dealing with armed struggle. Mondlane thought so too, for he says: 'the resolutions re-affirm the need for an armed struggle and the importance of simultaneously developing those areas which, as a result of armed struggle, came under our control'.[48]

It has become the sad lot of certain movements engaged in armed struggle to dwindle and peter out after an initial spurt. The people become demoralized and one of the sources of this demoralization are the frequent splits in the organizations. This is because the aims of the movement were not properly understood and the strategy of guerrilla warfare was not properly defined. After Frelimo had launched the armed struggle, few understood the direction of the struggle. In fact after one or two victories over the Portuguese, the population came out with flags thinking that independence had now come to them. On this score, the resolutions showed that Frelimo had assimilated the experiences of the protracted wars in China, Vietnam, as well as in Angola and Guinea Bissau. The resolutions also showed that they were able to apply these experiences to the specific conditions of Mozambique.

Firstly, the resolutions made it clear that the war in Mozambique would be a protracted one, and that there could be no quick victory. But victory was possible in the end, provided the entire population was mobilized. The resolution thus states: 'Our struggle is a people's struggle. It requires the total participation of all the masses of the people. For this reason it is necessary to intensify the mobilization and organization of the masses in the liberated zones, as well as in the regions where the armed struggles have not yet started. The direct participation of all in the armed struggle is, therefore, one of the main objectives of the people's mobilization effort.'[49]

Debray in his 'Revolution in the Revolution' minimizes the role of the militia in guerrilla warfare. On the other hand, the Vietnamese today regard the role of the militia as crucial and in many cases decisive. That is due to the high degree of politicization in the country, and their combat experience. They have ceased to regard its role as auxiliary. The Second Congress of Frelimo, however, adopts the middle position for a resolution reads: 'The organization of people's militias is an important form of integrating the masses into the armed struggle. In this way, at every place, sufficient and militarily prepared forces are created. People's militias are therefore reserve forces.'[50]

The broad tasks of the militia were laid down as production, vigilance and defence. In the liberated areas their tasks were specified to be that of: (1) transport of material and the sick; (2) reconnaissance and patrol; (3) fighting when the enemy invades the region.

After the armed struggle was launched, there arose differences between the civilian leaders who first of all worked underground and later in the civil administration, and the military cadres. The former were older, the latter being younger were trained in countries like Algeria and socialist countries. Here they came into contact with the most advanced political and military ideas and had first hand contact with those who had fought and had won freedom through armed struggle. The differences would arise on spheres of influence. The older men would resent having to take orders from young people, while the younger men would believe these older leaders were playing it safe and not risking their lives. These points were clarified by a resolution which said: 'Our war is essentially a political war and its direction is defined by the party. The people's army is part and parcel of the party, and its strategic plans are made by the top leadership of the party. In order to conduct correctly the struggle, all the leaders should be involved in the armed struggle. Only in this way, following the struggle step by step, the leaders can be able to solve all the complex problems arising daily. The people's army performs its task in accordance with the policy defined by Frelimo.'[51]

Mondlane's view that women should be more fully involved in the struggle was seen in the resolution calling for the creation of a women's detachment whose main functions were outlined as follows: (1) mobilization and organization of the masses; (2) recruitment of young people of both sexes to be integrated into the armed struggle; (3) production; (4) transport of material; (5) military protection for the populations.

The resolutions on the administration of the liberated zones aim at establishing people's power, for only through an adequate administration would it be possible to consolidate the defence of the liberated zones. In these, promotion of the economic and social progress of the people was stressed, in order to lay the basis for a victorious development of the revolutionary armed struggle for national liberation. On national construction, it was agreed that the liberated zones should constitute the material basis for growth of the revolutionary armed struggle for national liberation. In that sense the development of production assumed special importance.

The resolutions on foreign policy show Frelimo regarded its struggle as an integral part of a worldwide movement against imperialism, and for a society free from the exploitation of man by man.

In this respect it is appropriate to quote Mondlane when he reported to the Congress on behalf of the Central Committee: 'As we said previously an important part of the technical and material support which Frelimo receives from friendly countries outside the continent comes from the People's Republic of China, the U.S.S.R., various socialist countries, and Cuba. . . . At this moment I would like to take the opportunity to express the gratitude of the Central Committee of Frelimo and the militants of the Mozambican people to the government and the people of the People's Republic of China on the tireless work of its citizens who have trained and continue to train many of our military cadres in the art and science of modern guerrilla warfare, developed and perfected by Chairman Mao Tse Tung, and for the material support which the Chinese people give us through the government of Tanzania.'[52]

This shows the growth and the political maturity of Mondlane. The Mozambican may go to the Western universities for degrees in arts and medicine, but the degree in guerrilla warfare, the real university of struggle, means delving into Mao Tse Tung, Ho Chi Minh, Giap and Truong Chinh. The Mondlane who left Syracuse University in the early sixties to take up the full time position as President of Frelimo was not the same Mondlane who delivered the major address at the Frelimo Second Congress. The academician had become a revolutionary.

Of the African countries mentioned for their support for Frelimo, Egypt, Zambia and Tanzania were specially singled out. Tanzania was thanked in particular for the aid given by TANU and the people and government of Tanzania, under the leadership of President Nyerere.

The assassination of Mondlane

OF all the leaders of the national liberation movements in southern Africa engaged in the armed struggle, Mondlane was perhaps the best known in the West. He was in contact with intellectuals of five universities either as a student or when engaged in research. After completing his secondary education in the Transvaal, he was admitted as a student at the University of Witwatersrand. After his expulsion, he went to the University of Lisbon. He transferred his studies to the North Western University of Illinois, Ohio, where he received a doctorate after his M.A. After doing some research at Harvard, he taught for a while at the Syracuse University. For a short period he was connected with the United Nations. During the time previous to the independence of Tanganyika, he was working in the trusteeship department of the United Nations Organization in New York, as a research officer in connection with information from Tanganyika, South West Africa and the British Cameroons. He often received letters, documents and petitions from various organizations from all the Portuguese colonies pleading that the United Nations take action against Portugal. Therefore if he took the road of armed struggle it was not as a result of ignorance, for he knew just what happened at the United Nations.

Mondlane was genial by nature, without any complexes, affable, and easy to get along with. Even after he formed Frelimo and launched the armed struggle he did not break his links with intellectuals from the West. What was self evident to the oppressed Mozambican was that there could be no other way out but armed struggle. He found that it was not so with his friends at universities and the 'liberal' establishments. They always argued against violence. However, Mondlane maintained contact with these layers because he knew that they could assist in their own way the liberation struggle. Ths people of Mozambique needed financial and moral help. It was also necessary to publicize this half forgotten war. For this purpose, he was able to call in the help of these friends. Undoubtedly Mondlane's nature was such that his starting point with human beings was trust. And it was here that enemy agents came through with bogus charities, funds and scholarships with the sole purposes of subverting the movement. But they did not get very far as can be seen with his polemic with the students. Thus while Mondlane leaned more and more on the socialist countries for financial and material help, he appealed to the people of Western countries to give at least moral support. At a time when he had his hands full with political and organizational problems of Frelimo, he still found time to deliver a lecture to the students of Oxford University where he presented a historical account of the rise of Frelimo. There he also elaborated its aims and broad strategy.

A section of imperialists believed that sooner or later, Mondlane would realize the horrors of armed struggle and would return to the fold. There would be a seat at a university waiting for him, or his old UN job, should he throw in the towel. He was educated by the West and therefore they made a point of keeping in touch with him. What they hoped to achieve with him was what they succeeded in doing with Holden of UPA of Angola. The latter allowed the CIA in, and in a few years his movement was in a shambles. So much so that the OAU decided to withdraw recognition of it. But imperialism had not reckoned with Mondlane's passionate desire to see his people free. Furthermore, he had started a process from which he himself could not go back. The cadres and militants had been trained in an anti-imperialist tradition, and they would not allow easily any imperialist infiltration. What also made imperialist subversion difficult was the road that Tanzania had taken after its Arusha Declaration. By striking at finance capital, by nationalizing the commanding heights of the economy, it made it difficult for its agents to operate under the guise of experts and managers of banks and enterprises, the standard CIA practice.

The proceedings of the Second Congress of Frelimo shook them. Not only was Mondlane able to consolidate his position and put those who had been conducting a whispering campaign against him on the defensive, but he directed Congress towards understanding the nature of the People's War, as well as defining the tasks ahead. Congress had decidedly taken an anti-imperialist stand with NATO's role exposed. Further, Mondlane in their eyes committed the most unpardonable sin; he had brought Mao Tse Tung right into Frelimo. This was not true, but that is how they looked at it. Mondlane was too dangerous, and he had to be liquidated.

Further investigation will one day perhaps uncover just who was behind this dastardly plot. With the liberation of Mozambique and with the overthrow of the fascists in Portugal by the masses themselves, light could well be thrown on this assassination which shocked the conscience of mankind. Kavandame, a member of the Central Committee who later defected publicly to the Portuguese could well have supplied the PIDE with an account of the proceedings of the Frelimo Congress. The Western monopolists involved in the Cabora Bassa dam could have had a hand. Then there is the CIA. It could well have been a joint CIA and PIDE plot.

What has been suggested is that the book parcel was sent from West Germany and that it was sent also to Vice-President Marcelino dos Santos. However, the parcel to Santos arrived a few days late and the police noticed the similarity. Janet Mondlane who had been away raising funds in Europe, on arrival in Dar es Salaam after his death, said that it was the greatest tragedy in the freedom struggle in Mozambique. It was clear that Frelimo was faced with an international imperialist conspiracy aimed at destroying Frelimo through the assassination of its leaders.

Messages expressing sympathy, support and solidarity began to pour in from all parts of the world. These showed sorrow, grief and indignation at the dastardly attack. They extolled Mondlane as a revolutionary fighter. Others expressed confidence that Frelimo would continue to develop with unabated vigour.

Tanzania treated Mondlane, now dead, not as a freedom fighter, but as a head of state. President Nyerere ordered a 19-gun salute at the height of a funeral rite, and his casket was given an escort of honour composed of army officers. The funeral was attended by the Tanzanian President as well as the First and Second Vice-Presidents, TANU officials, ministers, as well as representatives from other liberation movements. Typical of the messages of solidarity and sorrow was one sent by Kenneth Kaunda, President of Zambia: 'The assassination of Dr Mondlane comes as a shock to my government and people of Zambia. Frelimo has lost a dedicated leader and Africa has lost a statesman. Dr Mondlane has brought to Frelimo not only stature, integrity and respect, but above all effectiveness in the struggle for the independence of Mozambique. Through his leadership Frelimo has become a force which the Portuguese administration could not but recognize as a determining factor in the future of the territory.'

Amongst others who sent messages were Presidents Sékou Touré of Guinea, Gamal Nasser of Egypt, Comrade Nguyen Tho, president of the Central Committee of the National Liberation Front of South Vietnam. The message of Kaid Ahmed, head of the FLN, was as pointed as it was significant. It said: 'The physical disappearance of Eduardo Mondlane does not mean the death of the movement he led with courage and wisdom. We are certain that the Revolution, far from dying will find in this painful proof the indispensable force which will allow it to overcome all blows directed against an African people.'

But the most moving and passionate tributes came from Mondlane's own comrades in Frelimo, firstly those who were with him when the idea of a national movement for Mozambique was still a dream, and secondly from others who grew under the umbrella of Frelimo. Amongst the latter were the flower of Mozambican youth who were rapidly acquiring manhood under the heat and stress of the Mozambican Revolution. For them Mondlane's death was the irreparable loss of a comrade, friend and teacher. They missed him at a time when they were most in need of his guidance. It is they who were able to reveal in their sorrow the maturity of Mondlane's character. The editorial of *Mozambican Revolution* January/February 1969 commented: 'He could understand and absorb the good of other civilizations and still never lose sight of the fact that the main goal was to turn this knowledge to the service of the Revolution.' On his organizational abilities it said: 'Out of the many tribes, he led a united front; out of the many tribes he was able to foresee one nation. Never did he indentify himself with one group or tribe. From him we learnt to judge a man on the basis of his ability and not his origin.' They also remembered how he taught them to be self reliant for, 'in dealing with the outside world, we saw in practice his concept of non alignment, based on the firm faith that it is not necessary to bend to any external power and that it is possible to work steadily towards the goal of reaching a political identity of our own. We praise him for having shown us the strength of relying on ourselves and trusting ourselves.' They remember how he told them again and again to 'know the enemy' for he said: 'Yes, we must kill, but not against the colour of the enemy. We fight against the things he fights for.'

Mondlane had sprung from a generation of freedom fighters and despite his long absence from Mozambique, he did not lose sight of the fact that he sprang from the people and was one of them. Yet he was able to move with ease with diplomats, professors and statesmen. The editorial noting this rare quality said: 'We thank him because he was able to speak for us, in the language of other men, the language of diplomats, the language of universities, the language of power. Among all these voices, he gave a voice to Mozambique, and imposing silence on others, he made that voice heard.'[53]

It is the wish of every revolutionary to die as he lived, in harness. When the book parcel exploded the enemy was jubilant, because they had liquidated another hated foe. But the Mondlanes, Moumiés, Ben Barkas, Pintos, and Lumumbas despite their assassinations can never perish, because they are children of the African Revolution and this Revolution is very much alive. As they fall, others rise to

E

take their place, and this is how Mondlane felt when he said: 'If I die, the Revolution will not be stopped, until my country is free.'[54]

Towards the end of his life, Mondlane was already thinking ahead of the society he would like to see arise after the destruction of the Portuguese colonial system. In fact he understood that the only moral right that he and Frelimo had to call on the Mozambican people to rise, to take up arms which would mean death, suffering and privation to thousands of Mozambicans, is that the society he intended building would be superior to anything the people had known for the past five centuries. This was reflected in the message of the Central Committee on the third anniversary of the launching of the armed uprising. He said that the purpose of the struggle is not to destroy. It is aimed first and foremost at building a new Mozambique where there will be no hunger and where all will be free and equal. He added: 'Since the point of the war is to build a new Mozambique, not just to destroy the colonial regime, we must all have ideas about how the future nation should be organized; but the issue is too far in the future for us to be able to discuss it formally at this stage.'[55]

He was, however, confident about this one thing when he said: 'The very fact that in over a fifth of the country the colonial state has been eliminated, has already radically changed prospects for the whole of Mozambique and perhaps even in the long run for the whole of southern Africa.'[56] The clock cannot be put back. The changes that have taken place cannot be reversed.

He died with this firm belief.

16

Class struggle in the Mozambican national movement

IF there is one consistent thread that runs throughout civilized society, since the introduction of private property, it is the class struggle. Private property in land, in particular, split the once homogeneous society into two hostile and irreconcilable camps, between those who possessed property and those who did not. Such has been the depth, scope and intensity of the modern class struggle between the proletariat and the bourgeoisie that it has continued even into socialist societies. Mao Tse Tung after twenty years of conquest of power in China says that classes exist in socialist society and the struggle has to be waged by the revolutionaries against those in authority taking the capitalist road.

It has been one of the favourite preoccupations of the ideologists of the bourgeoisie to put forward long winded arguments that classes are dying out and that the class struggle is something which is only of historical interest. And it is such ideas which African intellectuals trained in the Western universities have brought to Africa and have adapted to the particular African context. Therefore in Africa too, at a certain phase in the development of the national movements denial of class struggle became a fashion. These myths have been well and truly exploded by Kwame Nkrumah who in his book, 'Class Struggle in Africa' says: 'At the core of the problem is the class struggle. For too long social and political commentators have talked and written as though Africa lies outside the main stream of world historical development – a separate entity to which the social, economic and political patterns of the world do not apply.'[57] He continues: 'Class divisions in modern African society became blurred to some extent during the pre-independence period, when it seemed there was national unity and all classes joined forces to eject the colonial power. This led some to proclaim that there were no class divisions in Africa.'[58]

If class divisions were blurred in the early phase of Frelimo activity, it is only because class divisions had not developed as much as in China or India, where apart from the bourgeoisie tied to imperialism (comprador), there were also feudal landowners and the national bourgeoisie. The bourgeoisie, in the classical sense of being the owners of the means of production, is very weak in Africa. The indigeneous bourgeoisie here is the owner of property, land, houses, vehicles, and is tied to imperialism by a hundred threads. In Mozambique this class amongst the people was nonexistent. The owners of large plantations, mines, factories, and big property were foreigners or the Portuguese colonialists. Therefore, the concrete reality was that before the launching of the armed struggle the urgent problem was to weld the various tribes together into a single nation. And Mondlane did so in a practical way by launching the armed struggle which meant fighting together for common ends.

But as Le Duan, First Secretary of the Vietnamese Workers' Party has pointed out, in summing up the experiences of the Vietnamese Revolution over a period of fifty years, there could be no classless national Front. There could be no Front of the people. Either it is led by the workers in alliance with the peasantry or it is led by the bourgeoisie, or petty bourgeoisie. Therefore the national struggle is in essence a class struggle, and sooner or later liberation movements will be faced with it. The reason is that different classes who compose the Front have their own conception of what is to be the end of the struggle, and want to steer the struggle along the lines which would best suit their interests.

Frelimo was a Front consisting of peasants, workers, and the petty bourgeoisie. A section of the last grouping consisted of students. All had joined Frelimo having different long term objectives. These were not expressed when they joined, but showed themselves in the course of the struggle. As far as the workers and peasants were concerned, the elimination of Portuguese colonialism would not be enough. Their demands would only be realized if the system of exploitation also ended. But there were other people, including a few leaders, who saw in the struggle the path to fulfil their ambitions where by being ministers or top civil servants, they would be in a position to accumulate property. They saw it happening elsewhere in Africa, and they believed that it would happen in Mozambique as well. They would become what Kwame Nkrumah has described as the 'Party nouveaux riches'. Some of them went ahead and used their positions for this purpose. Then there was also a small layer of students who at the colleges and universities were frequently referred to as the future leaders of their people by their lecturers and really believed they were the elect. Thus without contributing one ounce of work to the liberation movement, they thought it was their divine right to ask for privileges as well as exemption from participating in the work of the liberation movement.

Mondlane in his polemic with the students in 1967 was aware of a polarization, expressing itself in political questions, but in the last analysis showing class alignment. He saw that the expression of student rebellion was a symptom of a larger issue. The students were being pushed into the frontline and expressing views of a much bigger and stronger force. In asking privileges for themselves, they were in fact preparing the ground for a stronger but as yet hidden force. Recognizing this incipient and unhealthy trend he said: 'In many respects, a greater danger lies in the formation of new African privileged groups; the educated as opposed to the uneducated ... once the people with power in a country enjoy a privileged economic position, they cease to share the problems that they are responsible for solving.'[50]

However, it was when the provinces of Cabo Delgado and Niassa fell under the control of the liberation forces and the National Front became the government, that the various groups showed their hand. The problem of government posed the question of 'whose government and whose power?' It also posed the other question of what sort of society the national movement wished to create in place of the old. There were two tendencies and these were shown to be the two directions Mozambique could follow. Should the overthrow of Portuguese domination lead to the establishment of a capitalist government where the small Mozambique elite from the educated and the petty bourgeoisie steps into the shoes of the colonialists, or should the direction be the elimination of exploitation of man by man?

Mondlane in reply to some of his Western friends as well as critics who wanted to know whether the goal of the

Mozambican struggle would be communism had said: 'Our state will not be a state like Russia or China. It will be a modern democratic single party state. Our model will be the neighbouring state of Tanzania. They have a challenging experiment under way and as far as I am concerned personally, Tanzania is providing that kind of leadership that all of us, south of the Sahara should want to know more about.'[60]

Before final confrontation takes place, classes wage their battles through ideas. And ideological conflicts on political economic, or even social matters can in the last analysis be traced to class. Of course, the exact definition of which ideas represent which class can be obscured. For example, during the Reformation in Europe the ideas of the bourgeoisie in their struggle against feudalism took a religious form. In Mozambique the form was racial, in that the fight was against the white man. Outwardly there could be nothing wrong with it, for in the experience of the Mozambican worker and peasant, the white man was identified as the plantation owner, the top official, the owner of the big factories and mines. The people had come to identify, from their own experience, the white man as the symbol of oppression and exploitation. Conversely, they believed that the blacks could not be exploiters and oppressors because they had no practical experience of this. Frelimo, realizing this was a wrong conception, began a process of education designed to clarify the nature of oppression and to expose the real enemy.

But the aim of those who whispered the ideology of racialism was to turn the national struggle into a racial war. The intention was to throw dust on the vital question whether the new Mozambique would end exploitation, or only white exploitation, and replace it with black exploitation. To pose the latter sharply would mean incriminating themselves and showing up that they stood for exploitation. Friends also saw in this an attempt to discredit Mondlane and Santos because they had both married white women. Mondlane looked at it in another way. For he was determined that the Frelimo struggle should not be turned into a racial war. Even those in

118

the West who opposed the armed struggle conceded that the Frelimo society of the future would be a just society, for there would be no discrimination based on colour or race.

The Mozambican struggle was part of a larger struggle against imperialism. Not only independent African states, not only socialist countries, but radical and progressive layers in the West had rallied to the Mozambican cause because the People's War had been presented as a just war, and the goal of sovereignty and independence where every Mozambican would have equal rights, irrespective of race, colour and creed, a just demand. All those who supported Frelimo in their own way knew that Mondlane would never be a party to a situation where in the new Mozambique the majority would oppress and discriminate against a minority on the basis of colour. Here Mondlane had in mind the example of Tanzania, where privileges were being taken away from people not because of their colour or race, but because they stood for exploitation. The Mozambican struggle received support precisely because it stood to end exploitation and oppression. But the sources would dry up if it was known that the society Frelimo intended to create stood for exploitation of the majority by the minority.

Mondlane entered into the ideological arena to fight these pernicious ideas. In a series of speeches he defended the view that Frelimo was fighting the Portuguese not as a race, but because they were oppressors and exploiters. He wanted those who held opposite ideas to come out in the open and to defend their standpoint. They did not do so openly.

Polarization of those who held these ideas, identifying themselves publicly with the exploiting classes, was not evident during Mondlane's life. Mondlane thus looked at it as an erroneous view, which though dangerous, could still be corrected. It was only after Mondlane's death that these ideas were seen to belong to a particular class which was springing up on Mozambican soil and which stood for exploitation. A feature of the growth of Frelimo was its success in achieving in a few short years progress which had taken others decades to accomplish. With such rapid growth it was to be expected that not all would be able to keep pace with this rapid development. Some people began to fall by the wayside, particularly the generation which still believed in a constitutional struggle. 'Some Mozambicans, looking at the example of African countries idealized the realization of independence in the halls of the UN in talks and negotiations which would result in the handing of independence by the Portuguese government to Frelimo in a solemn ceremony with feasts and celebrations. When it became clear that that method had failed, and recognition came of the necessity for armed struggle, those Mozambicans who were not psychologically prepared for an armed struggle (who were the majority of the founding members) deserted the organization. Then there were those who accepted the armed struggle, but who believed that Frelimo should wage a conventional battle, achieve a decisive victory at one go, and expel the Portuguese. Such a people did not understand the nature and protractedness of the People's War. They too lost heart, left Frelimo, thereby to fade into oblivion.'[61]

In these cases, one is dealing with desertions by a section of the petty bourgeoisie. It is unstable as a class, and subject to pressure from the enemy classes. It hates the rulers, and fears the masses. If there was any struggle, it was one to hold them for as long as possible in Frelimo.

However, it was the group inside Frelimo who believed that the Mozambican struggle should aim to expel the Portuguese, and that Mozambicans take their place without altering the structure and pulling down the oppressive and exploitative state machinery that posed the first real threat to Frelimo. For the struggle was within, and involved members of the Central Committee of Frelimo. These, once unmasked, showed that they stood for capitalism and the continuation of the system of exploitation. After Mondlane's death these elements showed their true colours. They who said that the war was to be against the white man in fact deserted and went over to the Portuguese, who used them to discredit Frelimo. Thus their anti-whiteism was just a cover to hide their class objectives. The leader of the group was Lazaro Kavandame. It was with him that the Vice-President of Frelimo, Simango, formed an unprincipled alliance.

The group decided to show its hand after the assassination of Mondlane. This was the period when the rank and file in Frelimo were demoralized and disillusioned. The new leaders were feeling their way. The editorial of the 'Mozambique Revolution' a year after Mondlane's death looked back and gave a frank and honest account of the wave of despair that swept the organization infecting every layer of the Front. It said: 'Sorrow and confusion fell over the combatants and the people. Uncertain, they questioned themselves on how that had been possible; disconcerted – they wondered whether the organization really contained such weak points within itself. The militants felt that a sudden heavier responsibility had been cast on to them; the people requested explanations and clarifications. For weeks the military offensive came to a halt; the militia ceased cultivating; the population stopped transporting vital material. Each of us questioned the future of the organization and the fate of the struggle.'[62]

Kavandame belonged to the same generation as Mondlane in that he matured politically and began his activities before the founding of Frelimo and the launching of the armed struggle. Before the founding of Frelimo, his intellectual horizon did not go beyond the economic level. While his counterpart with similar ideas in the urban areas would establish trade unions, he founded a cooperative society of cotton growers. One of the members described the cooperative and the role of Kavandame. He said: 'We had only a few people in the first year, and then in the second year we cultivated cotton. We called our cooperative the Mozambican African Voluntary Cotton Society ... that was in 1957 ... and our cooperative developed. Many joined; and so the Portuguese company (in Mueda) got short of labour, and we began selling our cotton even to that company. We leaders worked hard and voluntarily; we took no percentage of the crop, we had no profit in money. All we leaders had our own shambas for our own support. Then the Portuguese Company complained to the authorities that our cooperative was really an anti-Portuguese political organization. In 1959 the leader, Lazaro Kavandame, was arrested and sent to Porto Amelia. But we weren't demoralized; we continued. Then the massacre occurred and they banned our cooperative movement. At the end of 1960, Lazaro came back.'[63]

Lazaro Kavandame himself relates how he came to join Frelimo. After the massacre at Mueda he realized that the Portuguese oppressors should be driven out. He relates: 'After a long and important discussion we reached the conclusion that the Makonde people alone could not succeed in driving out the enemy. We then decided to join forces with Mozambicans from the rest of the territory.'[64]

The cooperative springing from the people was a progressive move but, as Mondlane rightly remarked, cooperatives like trade unions could never in themselves unite the broad mass of the people to achieve independence. Further, functioning within the framework of the capitalist economy, there is little doubt that sooner or later it would also become enmeshed within the capitalist system.

Far sighted sections of the bourgeoisie allow trade unions and cooperatives to flourish, and then undermine their vitality by bribing the leaders and corrupting them. Thus the leaders, instead of fighting for the workers and peasants, become staunch upholders of law and order. But under the Salazar régime, trade unions and cooperatives were viewed with suspicion, and when Kavandame was detained his only offence was that he was the leader of the cooperative. His detention turned him into a hero and he was able to acquire a personal following.

When he entered the political movement he did so not as a Mozambican, but as a member of the Makonde tribe. And he did so because he believed that the Portuguese system would not offer him any security in the activities he was pursuing.

His rise in Frelimo was rapid. He became Provincial Secretary of Cabo Delgado Province and was in the Central Committee of the body. The liberation of the Cabo Delgado Province was to him the realization of his dreams and aspirations. What he had failed to achieve under the Portuguese, he had achieved in Frelimo. Not only was he in charge of the cooperatives which his position as Secretary of the province made possible, but he was also in charge of the export and import trade for this province.

In the liberated area it was understood that while private ownership of the farm (shamba) was not barred, there was to be no hired labour. This was regarded as exploitation, and certainly no leader of Frelimo was allowed to engage in this. In fact Frelimo leadership stressed cooperative development. Kavandame got round this in a clever way. He gave shambas to various peasants. In this way he was not in any way going against Frelimo policy. But this was just a front, for in fact these men were only nominal owners. They were in fact being paid by Kavandame, and their position was therefore that of hired labourers. Because he was very powerful in the area, he believed that no one would point a finger at him.

There was another way he also exploited his fellow peasants. As he was in charge of exports and imports for the region he charged whatever prices he liked. And this operated against the peasants, for he paid them low prices for their produce and charged them high prices for imported goods. In this way Kavandame was not behaving differently from the small traders, and even certain nationalized concerns in socialist countries, which exploit the peasants similarly in order to show a profit in their annual reports. The peasants protested and the people complained. They did not see any difference between Frelimo and Portuguese rule.

Thanks to the political consciousness of the cadres, this matter was raised in Frelimo itself and it went right to the Central Committee. Accusing fingers were pointed at Kavandame. It was said that what he had failed to do under the Portuguese – that is to promote his own economic advancement – he was attempting to achieve in the liberated areas. And it was not only Kavandame. Others like him were beginning to spring up in the liberated areas, waiting for the right moment to choke the Mozambican Revolution. Such was the overwhelming evidence against Kavandame that the Central Committee of Frelimo appointed a committee to investigate the allegations against him. The terms of the committee were narrow. It was to investigate the charge that he used his post in the commercial section to serve his personal interests, and exploited the people.

Kavandame organized to prevent the committee from doing its job. He did not scruple to get his henchmen to commit murder. Comrade Samuel Kankhombe, Deputy Chief of the Operations Section of the Defence Department was killed. On 3rd January 1969, the Executive Committee of Frelimo after considering the case against him dismissed him from his post as Secretary of Cabo Delgado, as well as head of the Frelimo commercial section. He also lost his position on the Frelimo Central Committee. Mondlane died on the 3rd of February 1969 and in April, two months later, it was publicly announced that Kavandame had defected to the Portuguese.

It then became clear that Kavandame had been following a deliberate line, not only politically but also militarily. Thus it was he who peddled the idea that the struggle was against the white man. He and his group also opposed the military strategy of Frelimo, which provided that after the Portuguese were cleared from one area, the guerrilla forces should move into another area in order to liberate it. It was his opinion that all the Frelimo forces fighting in the different provinces should concentrate in one province, which of course would be Cabo Delgado in which he had complete control. In short what he was visualizing was 'Uhuru' for Cabo Delgado and for the Makonde tribe instead of for Mozambique as a whole. He was in fact asking Frelimo to create a Bantustan in Mozambique. The views of Kavandame and his followers were defeated.

It is possible that Kavandame was in contact with the Portuguese even before his final desertion. For with his defection, it was known that the Portuguese gave him a reward of 50,000 escudos.

The Portuguese believed that with Kavandame's desertion, the whole of the Makonde tribe would lay down their arms, and this would break the backbone of the resistance. The Portuguese authorities decided to capitalize on the situation to the extent that Salazar's successor, Caetano even went on television for a 'family talk'. The betrayal of

Kavandame was hailed as a great success for Portugal and he invited Mozambicans to join him to construct a multi-racial society. He said: 'The same peace we offer to all those who sincerely renounce war and who want to cooperate in the great, attractive task of building the Portuguese multi-racial society.' He described the traitor, Kavandame, as a principal chief of the Makonde tribe and said, 'the chief had realized that the rebellion was unjust for Portugal and inconvenient for his own people. He returned like a prodigal son and was welcomed joyfully'.[65]

The Portuguese had believed that Kavandame would be able to bring a large section of the Makonde people with him because of his prestige. But in this they were mistaken. Only seven people followed him on the slippery path of betrayal. The reason for this was that, in the course of the armed struggle, there had been a growing politicization of the masses. If Kavandame was a hero in 1959 because he was arrested, now it was no longer the case. The new heroes were the guerrillas who had no property, who had only the sky as their roof and who went about, toiling, tilling, or fighting the enemy with almost empty stomachs. Kavandame, as one who was growing fat on the sweat of other people's toil, was now looked upon differently. He was seen not as a hero anymore, but as an exploiter. Kavandame, who stood for exploitation, thus joined the Portuguese who also stood for this very system. That is why Caetano was correct when he said, 'the prodigal son had returned home'.

Kavandame showed his true colours also as a tribalist. His association with Frelimo had not changed his political outlook in any significant way. In an interview publicized by the Portuguese he said that Frelimo was using the Makonde tribe as a scapegoat in the war against Portugal. He took the liberty of informing his masters that Frelimo was being supplied with arms from the U.S.S.R., the People's Republic of China and other 'communist countries'. The liquidation of Kavandame and his clique meant the victory of the revolutionary line over the reactionary line. It meant a victory of the line orientated towards the peasants and workers over the bourgeoisie.

Analysing the various differences of groups within Frelimo, the Central Committee made an assessment. It said that Kavandame's attitude and mentality were typical of the group to which he belonged. 'He opposed the strategy of protracted war. We thought that his position stemmed from ignorance. But then we started receiving complaints from the people of Cabo Delgado that they were being exploited. The value of goods they received from Frelimo were scandalously disproportionate. These accusations were directed against Kavandame. It was not ignorance. Kavandame and his group had a precise objective when they demanded the independence of Cabo Delgado alone. What they wanted was to substitute themselves for the Portuguese colonialists in exploiting the people.'[66]

The ideological struggle had this beneficial effect. It resulted in Frelimo clarifying the purposes of the armed struggle. Thus the aims of the revolution were laid down not only as independence and the destruction of the colonial system, but also as the establishment of a 'government based on the people, and for the people'. Comrades mobilized the masses politically, and explained to them what was at stake. The result was that the people learnt to know clearly who the enemy was, the enemy being defined as whoever in a certain movement believes in the exploitation of man by man.

The ideological struggle cleared once and for all the vital question as to which class should dominate the liberated areas. Should it be the toilers and tillers, or the bourgeoisie? It was this internal contradiction which, if allowed to continue for a longer period, could well have wrecked the organization. It was solved with the workers and peasants emerging victorious. Out of this struggle then, a new and higher unity was born.

But the bourgeoisie is not completely crushed so easily. At every stage, the class struggle will appear in different guises. In Kavandame, the bourgeoisie chose a fool who had no real following after his open methods of exploitation which discredited him in the eyes of his followers. Later, ones would arise who could be much more sophisticated. They would stand for the ideas of the bourgeoisie without themselves being involved in open corrupt practices. In such cases it would be difficult to detect them. Or those who decide to take this road might be important persons, who in the past rendered valuable services to the struggle. Such a person, unlike Kavandame, who only looked to his tribe, would find and organize support for his views, in the whole of Mozambique. Vigilance and more vigilance is needed, not only in Mozambique but in the whole of Africa.

The experience of the People's Republic of China is relevant here. Victory in the struggle against imperialism and the comprador bourgeoisie and the feudal landlords took almost thirty years. For another fifteen years, the people, after having emerged victorious, were involved in the task of socialist construction. Yet even on this soil the bourgeoisie appeared with Liu Shao Chi as its spokesman. And Liu had rendered yeoman service to the Chinese Revolution. Even his theoretical contributions were such as to be quoted by Mao Tse Tung. He was regarded as one of the senior men in the top leadership of the Party. Yet after almost forty-five years of service to the Revolution he took the line which would have deflected the revolutionary path of the Chinese and have led to the restoration of the bourgeoisie. It was clear that despite the road to socialism in China, the habits, thinking and aspiration to become bourgeois die very hard. To prevent society becoming infected any further, Mao Tse Tung unleashed the Cultural Revolution, where millions of workers, peasants, students and youth rose to denounce and crush those in authority taking the capitalist road. Even now, the struggle has not ended. However, with the experiences of the Cultural Revolution it will not be easy for any one to push China back to the road of pre-1949.

The new leadership of Frelimo knows that the victory over Kavandame, does not mean the utter defeat of all counter revolutionaries and the bourgeoisie. The smarter ones have retreated. From the soil of liberated areas with their low level of economic development, which Frelimo is trying to improve, the bourgeoisie will spring up once the climate is favourable. If they see a difference in the leadership then they will come in and try to drive a wedge to split the organization. This again calls for vigilance.

The Portuguese believed that with the death of Mondlane, followed by the betrayal by Kavandame, Frelimo would be split from top to bottom with leaders hurling not only mud against each other but hand grenades. Caetano hoped that where he had failed militarily he would succeed by open bribery. That is why the surrender of Kavandame was widely publicized. But he and others who wished this to happen were mistaken. Frelimo was 'Indisposed', but only for a while. The revolutionaries quickly diagnosed the cause of the malady and were able to take action before the rot spread. Like a healthy, young and virile body it not only recovered again, but also acquired a degree of immunity in the process.

A year after Mondlane's death, and with a higher consciousness as a result of the struggle, it could comment editorially: 'We have reached a higher form of unity and intensified the armed struggle. We have mobilized and organized new populations, killed hundreds of colonial soldiers, downed aircraft, sabotaged bridges and roads . . . we have increased production to such an extent that most zones are self-reliant on food . . . the heritage had not only been saved, but brought further on . . . out of Mozambican blood, shed for justice, new warriors spring up and their forces are multiplied with consciousness.'[67]

17

The role of the individual in revolution

MONDLANE was not the first Mozambican leader to be assassinated nor has he been the last. Similarly on a world scale, imperialism in its reckless desperation will resort even more and more to this method of eliminating leaders, as it loses grip on its former colonies. Thus attempts at assassination have been made on more than one occasion on Kwame Nkrumah, Sékou Touré, Obote and others. But in the Mozambican struggle, there has been a growing record of assassinations of its leaders. Thus even before Mondlane, James Siguake, whilst on a party mission was killed in Zambia, followed by Matheus Muthemba in Dar es Salaam, and Samuel Kakhombe also in Dar es Salaam.

The imperialists have a battalion of 'experts' who have studied the People's War and its military strategy of guerrilla warfare. This has been done in order to evolve suitable counter strategies. Some of these are barbarous and savage, like the one where they say, 'that the only way to save a city is to destroy it'. Just as savage and barbarous is their policy of assassination of the leaders of national liberation movements, and of working class leaders. This, however, flows from a completely mistaken belief that it is the leaders who make history, and that revolutionary movements will stop once a leader is eliminated.

Until the nineteenth century, history in fact was presented as the record of action of this or that leader, or the life of this or that king. It was a break from monotony when a religious leader appeared on the scene, and stole the historical limelight. This view of the role of the individual was, however, subjected to criticism by rationalist thought of the late eighteenth century and early nineteenth century. Thus Monod said: 'Historians are too much in the habit of paying attention only to the brilliant, clamorous and ephemeral manifestations of human activity to great events and great men, instead of depicting the great and slow changes of economic conditions and social institutions which constitute the real, interesting and intransigent part of human development. Most of the events which are called historical have the same relation to history as waves which rise up from the surface of the sea, gleam in the light for the moment and break on the sandy shore, leaving no trace behind them, have to the depth and constant motion of the tides.'

What Portuguese imperialism, as well as imperialism as a whole, pretends not to understand, or does not understand, is that as capitalism overthrows tribalism and feudalism it sets in motion processes and forces that will bring about its own destruction. These are laws operating in society with the same accuracy and logic as natural laws that for instance govern the movement of tides. And like the tides, they must flow inexorably, come what may.

But unlike the operation of natural laws which operate independently of man, the new historical school of thought places the creative role of man as the chief instrument of change. As Marx said in his famous thesis on Feurbach: 'The materialist doctrine that men are products of circumstances and upbringing ... forgets that circumstances are changed precisely by men and the educator himself must be educated ... men make their own history but do not make it just as they please; they do not make it under circumstances, directly encountered, given and transmitted from the past.'

The twentieth century opened up a historical era of colonial uprisings and proletarian insurrection, just as the French Revolution of 1789 opened the era of the bourgeoisie. The basis of these were laws of historical development which were operating independently of man. But there arose the Lenins, Ho Chi Minhs and Maos who were able to interpret these laws so as to change society. Thus they were able to lead the people correctly to overthrow their own oppressive and exploitative systems. They have become heroes for the oppressed and exploited, precisely because they were able to solve the great social needs of the times in the countries they were in. They were not born great, but they grew in stature and greatness as they participated in the historical process of bringing about social change. A leader, however able and powerful, might lose grip of a situation, slacken his pace, put forward ideas and indulge in activity that runs contrary to the mainstream of history. In such a case the historical stream pushes him aside and continues its course. Such has been the case of Kautsky, Chiang Kai Shek, Kambona and Kavandame. The West has undoubtedly produced men of talent and ability in recent times. But they never grow into 'heroes' precisely because they are not part of the main historical stream. In fact the role assigned to them is to block the onward course of this mighty movement. Presidents Johnson and Nixon of the U.S.A. have tried in Indo-China. They have been ignominiously pushed aside to be received by the historical dustbins. In such a situation even the most talented looks a fool, and a genius becomes a dullard. This is what awaits those who, like Canute, wish to stop the historical tide.

Thomas Carlyle calls great men 'beginners'. Plekhanov agrees, for he says: 'A great man is a beginner precisely because he sees further than others and desires things more strongly than others. He solves the scientific problems brought up by the preceding process of intellectual development of society; he points to the new social needs created by the preceding development of social relationships; he takes the initiative in satisfying these needs. He is a hero.'[68]

The educational institutions of the bourgeoisie, particularly the universities, have a role of corrupting the minds of students and indoctrinating them under the guise of freedom of thought. At best, the student leaves the university confused and muddled, and unable to distinguish right from wrong, friend from foe. It is in the school of struggle and of life itself that he has to unlearn what he had been taught at the university. Mondlane too went through this same process, and once his mind was clear, he was able to use his education as a step in the ladder to get at true knowledge. He thus transformed the education he received, after the proper cleaning process, to use it as a weapon in the service of the people, and against the oppressors.

His new knowledge, his vast experience, his contact with various layers of society made him see further than most of his contemporaries in Mozambique. Then there was his own temperament and nature, which while genial and accommodating, also contained a soul passionately determined to free his people. He saw more clearly than anyone else that the Revolution in Mozambique must come; and it was he who set it in motion. In doing so, Mondlane, a product of a particular social relationship, became a social force.

But Mondlane, like Lenin, Mao, Ho Chi Minh, Che Guevara, though heroic and farsighted, could not change the general trend and cause it to flow in the opposite direction. In fact their farsightedness lay precisely in recognizing the direction of the general movement of society and flowing with it in order to direct it towards certain goals. Mondlane in thus flowing with the general historical stream also directed it to specific goals. In this way he gave it his own individual stamp, and in this way, and in this sense, the individual does make history. Thus in Mozambique, he was able to form a National Front of the most diverse elements, and held it together until his death. Simultaneously with the movement's formation, he prepared for an armed struggle. He sought to integrate the intellectuals with the people, but at the same time fought the tendency that they should have any special privileges in the movement. He processed the ideas and practices of other liberation movements with such speed that what began as a guerrilla war of only 250 people was transformed into a People's War. His intellectual honesty and humility made him unafraid of self-criticism. He praised genuine friends even if it meant antagonizing others. Frelimo thus bears Mondlane's individual stamp and will continue to do so until the next phase of its development.

Mondlane participated actively in the process of change, and in doing so he himself changed. The Mondlane who had left Syracuse University in 1961 was not the same Mondlane who was laid to rest in Dar es Salaam in February 1969. He had grown in stature. Ideologically he had become clearer, his conviction deeper, and his cause dearer. The Revolution had made Mondlane. It had become his life and he died radiating its intensity.

18

Eduardo the man, as seen by his wife Janet

'MONDLANE was born of a polygamous family of chiefs. His mother, Chude, after whom their eldest daughter has been named, was a remarkable woman, for she was a warrior who fought alongside her husband. In her old age she suffered a great deal because she was periodically seized with a fear that the enemy was about to attack her. She would then dash off to the forest, with the young Eduardo. It was

Mondlane's first practical experience of the harsh and cruel life under colonial oppression, for it was his duty to journey to and from the village carrying food, water and other necessaries to the brave and gallant woman until she was normal again.

Mondlane's family regarded him as rather strange, for he wanted none of the privileges and ceremonies attached to chieftainship. He treated all as equals. However, when the call came the younger members of his family joined Frelimo. But once in the organization his relatives were all treated equally, because he wanted them to grow up fighting their own battles and not under his shadow, for he believed that this would make men of them.'

At his death Mondlane was survived by his wife Janet and three children, Eduardo Chivambe junior, Chude Jennifer and Nyeleti. The eldest was born in 1957, with Chude and Nyeleti following eleven months and three and half years respectively.

His first meeting with Janet was in 1951 when he was thirty-one and she seventeen. It was at one of the youth camps organized by the Church in the U.S.A. Eduardo had been in the country for only a month and had been booked to speak at a series of meetings. The object of this lecture tour was to make the people of the United States aware of what was happening in Africa, particularly in the southern part. Janet recalls: 'I found him a very interesting person and decided to marry him. You could say it was love at first sight on my part. On his part he did not notice me till the end of the session. It was the normal practice for us to move from one speaker to another in the panel, but after I heard him I just stayed through all his sessions. He was an extremely powerful person and a dynamic speaker who could hold the attention of his audience for hours. I told him that I would be writing a report of his speech and he said, "That's fine", and walked away. It was only after I informed him that I was seriously thinking of going to Africa to work as a medical missionary that he became interested. The last evening when all of us were supposed to be dancing we spent our time talking and talking. The next day when we were about to depart we exchanged addresses, promising to write. That is how it all began.'

Janet cannot recall much of what Mondlane said at the camp. Brought up in a family which was apolitical she could not understand much of what he said. In fact, all the politics she has now is what she acquired through her husband. But she remembers to this day that he said, 'There is a terrible thirst for education amongst the youth in Mozambique. The youth only know what the elders teach them. It is rare to find youth having new ideas. Traditional education has much that is good, and much that is bad, particularly those things not scientific, but based on superstition. These have to be eradicated if the youth is to grow up.'

They met again in 1954 never to be separated until his death fifteen years later. In between they had kept regular correspondence. Janet was keen on marriage there and then, but Mondlane insisted that she obtain her B.A. Degree first, for he did not think she would do justice to her studies with the additional responsibilities of the house and children which they had planned. They were married two years later, after her graduation. At that time Eduardo had completed his M.A. Degree and was working on a Ph. D. The subject he had chosen for his research involved a visit to the Congo. It was really a fascinating subject, said Janet, 'and everything was fixed for him to go. The Church had offered him the scholarship. But when they heard of our marriage, they unilaterally cancelled the scholarship, for they disapproved of such marriages. Nobody was in favour, and we fought a bitter battle for five years ... but we did what we thought was correct.'

Her parents finally came round. As early as 1953 they tried to dissuade Mondlane and had actually called him to the house where they raised the issue. It ended politely but did not alter anything. Janet, after marriage, refused to see her parents alone without her husband. Eduardo advised her to handle them gently so that they could adjust. According to Janet: 'after the birth of Eduardo junior my mother came to the house and the estrangement was all over. My parents changed a lot and they became extremely fond of the

134

children. They felt that my husband was some very great leader and were shocked at his death. It has been a great evolution for them.' She continued: 'For a while Eduardo worked at the United Nations. It was a desk job and he was never one for the desk. He thought that there was a lot of paper work which was unnecessary. However his job brought him into contact with Trust Territories including Tanganyika. Then he would work hard to help the petitioners with memoranda and would do research work for them. For this he was hauled up by his superiors, for as an international civil servant he had to be impartial.'

There was little time for romance, for according to Janet, 'he was a terrible studyer. We would go out for a drive or to the cinema now and then in his ramshackle car. But soon he was back at his books. After marriage there was little adjustment to make, for both knew each other's thoughts and feelings. Eduardo was extremely rational and seldom emotional. When faced with problems he would always weigh all sides and come to a decision even if it took several days. He was offered an interesting job by the Church. He considered it and finally refused because it would stand in the way of his going back to Africa.

For five years the Portuguese plagued him with tempting offers of a job. He was to be offered a professorship at Lisbon university and I too was offered one. Eduardo refused because he wanted to go back to Mozambique. There was one last desperate attempt when they sent a large amount of money as his first month's salary. Eduardo refused to accept it. He was asked to sign a rejection slip at the local Post Office but he knew their ways. He refused to do so, and told the authorities that he would not sign anything, and what became of the money was their own concern.

However, he would give way to anger. What maddened him was the bureaucracy which stood in the way of people getting help. The bureaucrats were supposed to help the people but would block efforts by asking for this or that form even when these were already supplied. He was impatient of those who believed more in paper than in people.

There were other incidents though rare when he lost his

temper. Students would pester him for scholarships. One such student was arrogant and said he would not move from the office until he was given one. Eduardo just held him by the scruff of his neck and threw him out of the door and told him not to come back.'

His friendship with President Nyerere was deep. Tanganyika in the fifties was a Trust territory, and it was in this period that he met the leader of TANU which was formed in 1954. Janet says: 'Their relationship was a close one for they agreed about people as human beings. Nyerere has the same enjoyment and the same attachment to people as Eduardo. Eduardo called himself a humanist, that is, he believed that human beings can change the world. Man does not have to rely on a force outside himself. He himself with others can change the world if he exerts himself. That is what President Nyerere believes. Both shared the fundamental belief that Man if given the right opportunity and the right education will do the right thing and make the right decisions. This was a real and deep belief. Education here means education in the broad and wide sense of having regard for others and not being selfish. That is what made Eduardo trust the peasants in Mozambique. You don't have to go to school to think in a logical way. A warm and deep relationship between people is rare. You have to have two special people for them to communicate with each other with such profound understanding. This was the case between Eduardo and President Nyerere because underlying this was the deep and fundamental belief in the value of a human being, and respect for him as a human being.'

It was well for Frelimo to have him as their head for he had qualities which could weld people together. According to Janet, the leaders 'hung round him' and that was useful in the early phase of the movement. People came from different areas and did not know each other. As in South Africa so too in Mozambique people did not trust each other, for if you have children who are hungry you could do anything. It was necessary to gain time in order to create a spirit of trust. He was able to gain that time by dint of his personality. People trusted him even if they did not trust each other.

Some leaders left because they were crooks. Once they were discovered they knew that not all the good things they did would save them, for they could not expect sympathy from their leader, although he gave every one a chance to redeem himself.

Kavandame was a real crook. I saw a letter written by Eduardo dated January 1969. It began this way: 'You and I have been together for a long time. It was very distressing for me to find these things (he had defrauded the peasants). Therefore I have to relieve you of your positions.' Eduardo took this hard for here was a human being who had just failed other people. There was no hatred, bitterness, or repression, but a terrible disappointment for failing the very people who had relied on Kavandame.

Eduardo was a great talker, and he could talk for hours. But he was also a great listener. He would listen for hours on end to anyone who had problems. That is why individuals came to him with their problems. It was not because he was a President and therefore wielded power but that he took a deep interest in the problems of human beings. His method in dealing with these things was simple. After listening to the complainant, he would call all those who had been mentioned to come together and to hear what they had to say. After that it was easy to find the cause of the trouble and also the solution. He laid down certain guidelines about work and these are followed still by Frelimo.'

Janet says: 'Eduardo had no strong attitude towards formal religion and demolished what I had not by a frontal attack but through discussions at random. Nevertheless, he recognized the Church as a powerful institution for it contained elements which were progressive and which would help the liberation movement. The children have been brought up in an essentially secular atmosphere, although it was felt that they should be given sessions of religious education. But with Eduardo junior the sessions ended in a fiasco. In New York he was sent to a Sunday school where the teacher told them of an all powerful God who was watching them all the time. Eduardo had nightmares for he thought of someone peering through his window at night. In Tanzania it was the same. On the one hand they were told that the damned would all go to Hell. On the other hand, examples were given of believers who, when their bus was stuck, just prayed and the puncture was miraculously repaired. Eduardo junior just reacted strongly and said: "Do you expect me to believe all this trash?" That was the end of his formal religious education.'

Eduardo loved his children deeply and this was reciprocated. There was a time when Chude was offered a scholarship to go to the Soviet Union. 'We debated and we decided not to send her because we could not part with the child.'

'We discussed a great deal about the future of our children. We decided that in the end we would tell them: "You do what you like, because that is what you will do best." Chude thus is being trained as a dancer. However, that is all within the discipline of Frelimo. Thus Mondlane took his son to the Frelimo camp for training as other Mozambican children of his age. When Chude arrived for a holiday from the U.S.A. she too had to go to the camp, although she would have much liked to be with her mother, and brother and sister. But at the end she was glad for, although it was hard, it was good.'

Mondlane was a product of a general historical trend of world revolution of which the Mozambican Revolution is an integral part. The bourgeoisie claimed him, for it was they who gave him education in their schools and universities, and they who offered him lucrative positions. But the current of Revolution was strong and it snatched him from the bourgeoisie. The rulers have to contend with the phenomenon that a few amongst its own class break from it periodically and cast their lot with the oppressed and exploited. Mondlane was one of these rare persons.

Appendixes

I

The Development of Nationalism in Mozambique

by Eduardo Mondlane

MOZAMBICAN nationalism, like practically all African national-ism, was born out of direct European colonialism. Mozambique's most specific source of national unity is the common experience (in suffering) of the people during the last one hundred years of Portuguese colonialist control. In order to understand the develop-ment of Mozambique nationalism, we have to study the main stages of development of Portuguese colonialism in our country and not the reaction of the people to these.

Before I outline these stages of the development of Portuguese colonialism and their relationship to the rise of nationalism, I wish to present a definition of nationalism. By nationalism I mean 'a consciousness on the part of individuals or groups of member-ship in a nation or of a desire to develop the strength, liberty or prosperity of that nation.' (The Chatham House Report, Royal Institute of International Affairs, 1939.) The above definition applies to nationalism in all circumstances or stages of develop-ment of any people. For instance, it might apply to European nationalism as a continental phenomenon, or French, American, Russian, Chinese, Brazilian, etc., nationalisms as expressions of the aspirations of given ethnic or national entities. The African context in which Mozambican nationalism finds expression might require further refinement of the definition offered above. In view of the recent historical circumstances which affected the lives of the various people within the continent of Africa, it is necessary to add that African nationalism is also characterized by the develop-ment of attitudes, activities and more or less structured programmes aimed at the mobilization of forces for the attainment of self-government and independence. In the specific case of Mozam-bique, shared by all Portuguese colonies in Africa and possibly by all other remaining peoples yet to be free, these attitudes, activities and structured programmes have to include the estab-lishment of military or paramilitary schemes for the final show-down before the actual attainment of independence can be assured.

If you could bear with me for a few more seconds in connexion with these preliminary remarks, I should like to sum up the definition of nationalism offered above in the following manner:

(a) a consciousness on the part of individuals or groups of membership in a nation – in our case, Mozambique;

(b) a desire to develop the strength, liberty or prosperity of that nation, – the concept of the Mozambique Liberation Front (or FRELIMO as we are popularly known) of the future socio-cconomic structure of the country and how to go about implementing it;

(c) the specific goal of attaining self-government and independence – FRELIMO's political and military programme;

(d) a concept of the people's unity – the Mozambican people's desire to rid themselves of Portuguese imperialism and colonialism so as to be completely free to develop their socio-economic structures as they wish; and,

(e) the establishment of more or less permanent political structures for the pursuit of national objectives in cooperation with other African nations.

In reference to African nationalism in general, it is necessary to stress four more points:

(i) that it is a reaction against political controls imposed by Europeans upon the African peoples; and,

(ii) that it is a reaction against foreign, especially Western, economic exploitation of the African natural and human resources.

(iii) In those areas of Africa where a combination of European and Asian populations have come to settle alongside of the African peoples, African nationalism has had to include also a reaction against local cultural and socio-economic barriers created by members of these non-African communities.

(iv) Concurrent with the rise of African nationalism, there developed another kind of nationalism, cultural nationalism, epitomized by the mushrooming of all sorts of theories of the African man, labelled 'African personality' by Anglophones and 'la Negritude' or 'Africanité' by Francophones.

Mozambique is one of the remnants of an old Portuguese colonial empire which was established during the sixteenth, seventeenth, eighteenth and nineteenth centuries in Asia, South America and Africa. In Africa the remnants of this empire still include Angola, Mozambique, Guinea (called Portuguese), the Cape Verde Islands and St. Tomé Island. The largest of these colonies is Angola, although Mozambique has the largest population of them all.

Contacts between Portugal and parts of what is now known as Mozambique began at the end of the fifteenth century, when Vasco da Gama, a well-known Portuguese navigator, reached the island of Mozambique in early March 1498. Since the main interest of the Portuguese kings who had sponsored these trips was to open a safer route to India than the then dangerous Near East land route, for many years the Portuguese satisfied themselves with establishing filling stations along the East African coast, thus leaving the rest of the interior untouched. The Portuguese claim that they have been in Mozambique for over 450 years, implying that for all that time they have been controlling our country politically. If there is any truth in this Portuguese claim, it has to do with the fact that soon after the first contact with the people of the coastal region of East Africa, the Portuguese, envying the wealth and power which the Arab rulers of the time possessed, they plotted, connived and organized whatever forces they could muster and fought their way into the position of control. This enabled the Portuguese to monopolize the then very rich East African trade in ivory, gold and other precious stones. In order to accomplish this, the Portuguese took advantage of the rivalries which then existed among the sheriffs and sheiks of such city states as Pate, Malindi, Kilwa, Zanzibar, Mozambique, Sofala, etc.; which were famous for their 'prosperity and elegance'.

At that time, wealth and cultural refinement were at least favourably comparable with the best in Europe and Asia. From the reaction of the Portuguese sailors of that time, gleaned from their diaries, it is possible to suggest that East Africa as a whole 'was a world comparable, if not superior, in material culture to Portugal in 1500'. (Duffy, 1962, p. 75.) However, political unity among these city states was then no easier than it is in the present East Africa. Let me quote Professor James Duffy: 'Political unity among these city states was a transitory burden. Each local prince defended his city's political and commercial independence, and at no time was there an East African nation, although the stronger towns at one time or another dominated their weaker neighbours'. (Duffy, 1962, p. 75.)

Even though the Portuguese took advantage of this unfortunate situation, they were never able to impose a lasting political control, except for a very thin coastal strip running from Cape Delgado to the city state of Sofala. By 1700 a resurgence of Islamic influence in this part of Africa had been able to effectively eliminate Portuguese traders and soldiers, as well as scores of towns which they had held from time to time. (Op. cit., p. 77.)

From the beginning of the eighteenth century, the Portuguese concentrated on conniving and cajoling their way into the control of the rich commerce of the area between Cape Delgado and the Zambezi basin, in an attempt to capture the flow of gold from the then famous gold mines of Monomotapa, which the Portuguese had believed to be the proverbial 'King Solomon's Mines'. Again, in this instance, the imperialistic activities of the Portuguese affected an area which included what is today known as Zambia and Zimbabwe or Southern Rhodesia. The capital of Monomotapa's empire was located in Mashonaland and was part of the Makalanga confederacy of that time.

During a period of 200 years, the Portuguese were able to derive a great deal of wealth by the simple fact that it had been able to control the flow of commerce from the interior of the country to the coastal city states and abroad. During the seventeenth and eighteenth centuries, Portuguese authority was firmly enough established in the northern and central parts of Mozambique so that it was possible to introduce Catholic missionaries, first, the Dominicans, then the Jesuits, who were the first to introduce Christianity in East Africa. However, whatever success this first missionary effort was crowned with, was almost completely destroyed in the eighteenth century by the corrupting effect of the marriage which had naturally resulted from the association of commercial, religious and political activities of the Church and the State. It was during this time that the *prazeiros* system was introduced in Mozambique. *Prazeiros* were Portuguese white and Mulatto settlers and landowners who, not unlike European feudal lords, ruled those Africans who had the misfortune to fall under their authority and control. Their lot was worse than that of slaves. These *prazeiros* often controlled whole districts as personal properties and recognized no law but their own, and only occasionally paid their vassalage to the king of Portugal. Jesuit and Dominican missionaries of the time also came to own vast tracts of land, administering it like any *prazeiro*, collecting head taxes and when slavery became more profitable, they dealt in slaves. It was out of the *prazos* system that the great land companies, such as the Nyasa and Manica e Sofala companies developed. It can also be presumed that at least the peculiarly Portuguese and heartless concessionary company system which typifies the major economic enterprises of Portuguese colonialism derived its refinements from the *prazos* system of this period.

Corruption in the *prazos* system was so rampant that by the third decade of the nineteenth century even the Portuguese government felt compelled to outlaw it. Among other reasons for its abolition by the Portuguese colonial government, the *prazos* system was notorious for fostering insecurity for person and property, and for the excessive number of Africans who were compelled to leave the area altogether due to the slaving practices of the manor lords. All of this resulted in the almost complete collapse of the Portuguese administration. However, in order to reimpose Portuguese authority, it was necessary to recruit the cooperation of some of the *prazeiros*, which meant their reinstatement; therefore, the vicious circle!

All along, however, the financial benefits which accrued from the slave trade were so great that the *prazos* of central Mozambique had become the reservoirs for slaving. It must be noted here, even in passing, that although the slave trade was one of the most characteristic Portuguese economic activities, slavery *per se* in East Africa was practiced long before Vasco da Gama touched this coast of Africa. Most of the slaves from East Africa were sold in the Middle East and in South East Asia, including India.

Most of the above colonialist-imperialist activities in East Africa took place primarily on the thin coastal strip, involving mostly contacts with the Arabs and the Swahilis, with only very superficial contacts with the bulk of the Bantu speaking people of present day East Africa and Mozambique.

It was with the proverbial scramble for Africa, which began in the second half of the nineteenth century, that we must date the start of the Portuguese conquest of what is now Mozambique. After the partition of Africa at the Berlin Conference of 1884–1885, Portugal was impelled to capture and solidify what had been dished out to her. In order to accomplish this, the Portuguese used every technique known in the history of colonial conquests. Where it was possible she used infiltration by Portuguese traders, who disguised tehmselves as simple businessmen interested in the exchange of goods between equals; but later on, after having thoroughly spied and mapped out a whole region, they invited their military forces in, which subsequently wiped out whatever resistance might have been put up by the local rulers. At times, the Portuguese used white settlers, who pretended that they needed land to farm, but who, after having been kindly accommodated by the naïve traditional rulers, claimed possession of the communal lands and forced their way to enslaving the African peoples who were originally their hosts. Sometimes even Portuguese missionaries were used as pacifiers of the natives, using the Christian faith as a lullaby, while the Portuguese military forces occupied the land and controlled the people.

143

Where the traditional political authority was strong and the military machinery was adequate to offer a serious resistance to European conquest, the Portuguese were more tactful, using techniques of initial contact which were more gentle. For instance, in these circumstances, the Portuguese were prepared to begin their contacts with strong African states by establishing diplomatic relations; sending Portuguese 'ambassadors' to the courts of the most important traditional rulers. Then after having sufficiently spied out the internal strengths and weaknesses of the government, they proceeded on to attack, using the traditional excuses of 'provocation' or 'protection of the security of the white settlers or missionaries', etc.

This is the way in which the war against the last of the Mozambican traditional empires, the Gaza Empire under Gungunyana, was justified. The war against Emperor Gungunyana began in 1895 and ended in 1898 with the death in battle of General Magigwane and the capture and deportation of the Emperor to Portugal, where he died several years later.

As to the kind of government which the Portuguese established after they subjugated all parts of the country, we have already described this in presentations which have been published elsewhere.

The Rise of a Mozambique Nationalism

As is clear from the foregoing, the success of the Portuguese in controlling the whole of Mozambique was due mainly to the lack of a cohesive political force to oppose them. Right from the first days of contact with the East African coastal city states in the fifteenth century, when the Portuguese were able, albeit temporarily, to defeat and control many of them, through the sixteenth, seventeenth and eighteenth centuries, when they captured the main commercial wealth of northern and central Mozambique, up to the nineteenth century, when they proceeded to conquer and keep the present territory of our country, the reaction of our people was fragmentary. It was a piecemeal reaction which encouraged a piecemeal conquest of our people. Even as late as the second decade of this century, in 1917 and 1918 to be exact, when the Makombe of the Barwe, in an attempt to re-establish some of the power of his legendary predecessor King Monomotapa, staged a successful revolt, his success did not last long, for it was not a national Mozambican uprising: it was confined to one or two tribal kingdoms. (See T. O. Ranger, St. Anthony's African Papers, II.)

Mozambicans had to wait for more than 45 years before they

could seriously challenge Portuguese authority. I am referring to the national liberation war, launched on the 25th of September 1964 by the people of Mozambique under the leadership of the Mozambique Liberation Front.

Between 1918 and 1964, a number of minor local tribal uprisings took place in various parts of Mozambique, but they were easily crushed by the Portuguese, and their leaders were massacred or deported to the islands or to Portugal.

As the colonial system became steadily and firmly established in the whole country, a small class of educated African peoples slowly emerged, in spite of very meagre educational facilities available to Africans as a whole. To these Africans, who were sometimes called *assimilados* or *évolués*, the Portuguese offered limited opportunities for social and economic advancement in the colonial system, but only sufficiently to make them useful as instruments of contact between the European administration and economic interests and the masses of the black people. Among these assimilated Africans, and some Mulattoes and most Europeanized Asians such as Goans, there are those who believe that their socio-economic and cultural future, or even that of the whole country, belongs to a perpetual attachment to Portugal. But most of the educated Africans have no such illusion. They have seen over the years how their own people have gradually become poorer as the white man became wealthier. The more the black people tried to press upon the European privileged positions in the socio-economic structure, the more stringent the Portuguese colonial laws became. This, of course, brought about more frustration among the African people, especially among those who had education comparable to the Europeans.

Some of this frustration was expressed in plaintive poetry, such as the following lines by Noémia de Sousa:

> 'Oh Africa, my motherland, answer me:
> What has happened to my bush sister,
> that she comes no more to the city
> with her eternal little ones
> (one on her back, one in her womb),
> with her eternal charcoal-vendor's cry?
>
> Oh Africa, my motherland,
> you at least will not forsake my heroic sister.
> She shall live in the proud memorial of your arms.'

Whenever the political climate in Portugal permitted it, the frustration was expressed in direct political journalism, openly voicing and defending the rights of the black masses, as illustrated by the success of the Albasinis in establishing *The African Cry* (*O Brado Africano*) in the early 1920s, as one of the first African weeklies in the whole continent. Although this paper is still in circulation today, and is still the only Mozambican African paper, it has been thoroughly emasculated by the fascist government of Salazar so that it no longer says anything meaningful.

Other forms of protest against the excesses of Portuguese colonialism and imperialism took the form of political or semi-political associations. In the beginning of this century, when the Portuguese themselves were groping about for a more democratic system of government, several African political groups arose, which later became political parties. But when Salazar finally established the present fascist system of government, these parties were wiped out, and in their place was substituted the present more racial and communal associations. I am referring here to the rise and fall of such African organizations as the *Gremio Africano*, which later became *Associação Africana*. For quite some time this African organization was the only Mozambican political grouping which served as the focal point of most African aspirations. When it was becoming clear to the settlers that the African people were rallying around one body against their interests, they connived with some of the leaders and helped to split them into two groups. This split resulted in the formation of another African organization in the early 1930s *O Instituto Negrófilo* (The Negrophile Institute), which when the fascists took over the government in Portugal was forced to change its name to *Centro Associativo dos Negros de Moçambique*. The membership of these two organizations seems to reflect a division of the African people into two groups: the Mulattoes tending to predominate in the *Associação Africana* and the black Africans dominating the *Centro Associativo dos Negros de Moçambique*.

However, since these two organizations are no more what one might call popular movements, they no longer serve any visible social or political purpose for the masses of the oppressed African population. They are at best bourgeois social clubs, often called upon by the government to shout their part in the martial chorus of allegiance to Salazar and his fascist régime.

Another kind of semi-social, semi-political organization which left some marks on the Mozambique political scene is the *Associação dos Naturais de Moçambique* (Association of Native-Born Mozambicans). The organization was originally meant for European-born white settlers. Consequently, for quite a long time it openly discriminated in its membership against the so-called non-Europeans. But since about fifteen years ago, it began to allow some members of other racial groups to join the association. In fact, during the mid-fifties the *Associação dos Naturais de Moçambique* developed a policy favouring social integration between the two major racial groups, with a view to preparing the people for a future autonomous Mozambique under Portuguese leadership. At one point during the last ten years, the organization launched a scholarship campaign to subsidize the education of some promising Africans in secondary and commercial schools. At first the government encouraged the efforts of this group, perhaps believing that its leaders were only interested in the social and cultural advancement of the African people; but when it began to note that there were some tendencies toward a more genuine Mozambican nationalism among them, the government took drastic steps to stop them. The government arrested all of the top leaders of the association and replaced them with fascist leaders and placed the whole organization under direct government control.

Lately we have received information indicating that in the *Centro Associativo* the President of the Executive Committee, Sr. Filipe Tembe, has been arrested and is now in prison, apparently for deviating from the official fascist line set by the Salazar government.

The Rise of Political Parties

It was only after the second world war that political parties began to emerge on the Mozambique horizon. Since this was the case in practically all of Africa, I need not try to explain why it was so. Most of these parties, however, developed outside of Mozambique, in view of the fascist nature of Portuguese colonialism. About the only exception to this rule is the development of the Mozambique student movement, *União Nacional dos Estudantes de Moçambique* (UNEMO), which right from its inception had a definite political concern. This student movement began in Lourenço Marques in 1949, when a group of university students who were attending school in South Africa got together all the African students who were in secondary schools in that city and organized a group called *Nucleo dos Estudantes de Moçambique* (Nucleus of Mozambican Students). Even though this group had been established within one of the African associations referred to above, when the government began to sense its political inclinations, it pounced on its leaders, put them in prison and proceeded to try to purge it of all political connotations. I had just been thrown out of South Africa by the Malan government at that time, and having been one of the founders of *Nucleo*, I was also put in prison and thoroughly investigated by the State Police (PIDE).

The present Mozambique Liberation Front (FRELIMO) arose out of the merger of the three major political parties of Mozambique, which, in June 1962, decided to join into one movement. The three parties were: *União Nacional Democratica de Moçambique* (UDENAMO), which was first organized in Southern Rhodesia by Mozambicans working in that country; Mozambique African National Union (MANU), organized by those Mozambicans who had been working in East Africa; and *União Nacional Moçambicana de Independencia* (UNAMI), first organized in Malawi.

Since both the history and programme of the movement have been dealt with by me in other publications, I need not repeat them here, except to underline the following facts:

(1) FRELIMO is the only popular nationalist movement for the liberation of Mozambique;

(2) FRELIMO has one definite goal, the complete and unconditional liberation of our country with a view to developing it politically, socially and economically for the benefit of all the people of Mozambique as part of the total liberation of all the peoples of Africa;

(3) FRELIMO is a part and parcel of Africa, therefore, it adheres to all the programmes and policies of the Organization of African Unity; therefore, being the only Mozambican nationalist movement supported by the OAU through the African Liberation Committee, it cooperates with this body and all other African nationalist movements for the liberation of all of Africa;

(4) FRELIMO is part of all the progressive forces now guiding the revolutionary programmes of southern Africa. In this connexion, it must be pointed out that FRELIMO is now in the vanguard of all the southern African revolutionary forces now engaged in actually driving out the last vestiges of colonialism and imperialism in Africa.

At this stage one might ask: What is the reason for the present unity among the Mozambican people? Is this unity a durable one? In order to answer these questions we have to return to the definitions presented earlier in this paper and affirm that there is a Mozambican nationalism which unites all the various peoples of the vast territory from north to south, regardless of their languages, religions, races and cultures. In other words, there is now a consciousness on the part of the people of our country of belonging to a nation – Mozambique, and a desire to develop the strength, liberty and prosperity of that nation. The Mozambican peoples, after many years of facing a common enemy, have coalesced into one solid people, ready to free themselves from bondage. The Mozambican people have come to consider themselves a nation in the same way that the peoples of India, China, the Soviet Union and other multi-linguistic and multi-religious societies now consider themselves one nation.

It was mainly in the last 75 years that the Mozambican peoples learned their lesson in unity. Immediately after destroying our traditional rulers, the Portuguese confiscated our land and natural resources, putting them under the control and direct use of larger European economic interests, and harnessed our man-power for the benefit of these interests and the European settlers. The Mozambican national unity was born out of common experience in suffering together while working as forced labour on the large sisal plantations, while clearing thick forests for planting cotton, while picking cotton together, baling it, carrying heavy loads of it for hundreds of miles to the market centres monopolized by Portuguese and foreign concessionary companies, while sweating together, some with blood, cultivating peanuts, sugar cane and tea, or loading and unloading cargoes of these products and of heavy machinery from transoceanic liners to trains or vice versa for the benefit of Portuguese, South African, Rhodesian, European and American white interests. Mozambican unity was born out of toiling together in the deep, hot, narrow and dust-ridden shafts of the gold, diamond and coal mines of the Transvaal and Orange Free State to help enrich the South African and British Harry Oppenheimers and their American Engelhardts as they cooperate with the Portuguese to maintain a southern African economic empire for the white man stretching from the Katanga to the Cape. Our national unity was born out of the common experience of trying to escape together from Portuguese prisons, forced labour, *palmatoria* beatings and political persecutions.

After finding ourselves in all of these places and circumstances together for so many years, and in some parts of Mozambique, for so many centuries, we had no alternative but to unite into one solid people and organize a counter-force, the *Mozambique Liberation Front.*

Eduardo C. Mondlane
President
Mozambique Liberation Front

3 December 1964

149

2

The Crystallization of a Struggle for Freedom

by Eduardo Mondlane

I NEARLY felt flattered for being asked to address this conference especially after seeing the list of the individuals invited to speak. Such names, for instance, as Prime Minister Jomo Kenyatta, Vice-President Rashidi Kawawa, Kenneth Kaunda, venerable political names as they are, were matched against an unknown, me. But then I saw the name of my friend and fellow academician and United Nations officer, Bernard Chidzero, listed, and I concluded that you wanted me to reminisce on my academic past and the exciting years with the United Nations trusteeship system. I tried to see how that could have any relevance with a student seminar on East, Central and Southern Africa, whatever that means. On scrutinizing the programme further I noticed that my subject matter is to be 'The Mozambique Liberation Front', then I realized that it wasn't me they were really inviting but a representative of Mozambique, who must be a politician, with all the implications thereof.

I still feel flattered for the honour of representing my country in this seminar, but the role I must play is quite different from that of either an academician or an international civil servant. While as an academician I might have been forced to restrict myself to the narrow path of cold facts and their theoretical implications, as an international civil servant I might have been required to reduce whatever theoretical relevance there was in the situation in Mozambique to a restricted few, I am very glad that now as a politician I shall try to impart to you as much as possible the range of facts, theoretical implications and emotions.

Mozambique is one of the unfortunate few areas of Africa where independence will have to be won the hardest way possible. The reason for this is the fact that it is under the control of one of the most backward countries in the world: Portugal. In fact, Portugal, the nation which runs the affairs of our country today is itself not only under one of the most ruthless of modern dictatorships, but it's a colony of foreign capitalist interests. That is to say, the people of Portugal itself are not free. They are controlled by the Salazar fascist régime, which represents a number of economic interests holding stock in the wine, cork, cotton, sugar, rubber, shipping, diamond and cocoa industries. When you add to this a special Latin-Portuguese mentality or logic and the buttressing which all of this receives from the North Atlantic Treaty Organization, then you have one of the toughest colonial situations you could ask for. And that is Mozambique.

The *Mozambique Liberation Front* or FRELIMO therefore, is the organization called upon to shake up this whole situation and move the people towards not only independence, but also establish a system of government which will steadily direct them towards a more prosperous, just and happy life.

It might be necessary for me to give a brief outline of the geography and history of our country in order to enable some of you to understand what FRELIMO is facing.

Mozambique is a long coastal strip of land, with a coast-line of about 1,700 miles, a north to south stretch of 1,250 miles and an average east to west width of 400 miles, with a maximum of 718 miles in the Tete area, and a minimum of 56 miles in the Lourenço Marques area. Most of the country is within the coastal strip which is rather low and warm, while a small proportion falls in the plateau of the interior which has a comfortably mild climate. While the interior plateau is a grassland in which thousands of wild animals graze, the coastland alternates between the thickly forested north and the progressively thinning bushland of the south, with patches of sandy areas here and there. Agriculturally the north and the centre are fertile and rich in minerals of all kinds, including bauxite, oil, coal, cobalt, and gold.

The population for Mozambique is estimated at 7 million, including 100,000 Europeans, 35,000 Asians, 25,000 Coloured and the rest being of the Negroid stock. The most densely populated areas are the north and the centre, with an overall average density of 9 persons per square mile.

For many hundreds of years before the Portuguese colonialists occupied our country our people were organized in various linguistic and ethnic kingdoms whose economic base was mainly agricultural, with livestock as the mainstay.

The colonial history of Mozambique dates from the end of the fifteenth century when, in 1498, Vasco da Gama reached an island called Mozambique. However, for the next 300 years the relationship between Portugal and Mozambique was mainly commercial, for Portugal's main interest was India and the Far East. At that time the principal trading centres in East Africa were Pate, Malindi, Mombasa, Kilwa, Zanzibar, Pemba, the island of Mozambique and Sofala, all of which were populated by a combined population of Arabs and Africans, with a sprinkling of Persians and Indians. Also at that time, most of East Africa was part of an Indian Ocean commercial complex in which Arab, Indian and African goods were traded back and forth by middle-men who spoke a language very similar to the present-day Swahili. By the middle of the seventeenth century the Portuguese had been able to weaken, if not altogether destroy, the power of the various sheiks and princes who separately controlled the political and economic life of the coastal people. However, Portuguese authority never extended beyond a narrow strip of the northern part of the present-day Mozambique, plus a few coastal towns in what is now Tanganyika, Kenya and Zanzibar. In 1591 the Portuguese crown was forced to build the famous Fort Jesus at Mombasa, in order to strengthen her East African economic empire which was being challenged by the Arabs and Turks. During most of the sixteenth century Portugal practically monopolized East Africa's rich trade in gold, ivory and precious metals. The presence of Portugal in this part of Africa, however, confined itself to the equatorial region of the coast which included the northern coastal strip of Mozambique. The conquest of what is now called Mozambique did not take place until towards the end of the nineteenth century. The last wars against the encroach-ment of Portuguese colonial control over our country were fought between 1895 and 1917. Obviously, it was during the main period of the scramble for Africa, in which other European powers such as Britain, Germany, Italy, Belgium and France were busy imposing their authority over other African communities of East Africa and Madagascar, and Cecil Rhodes and his British–South African economic empire builders were grabbing the interior.

It is clear from the foregoing, therefore, that Portugal's claim of having controlled Mozambique for over 450 years has no foundation whatsoever. If anything it is a reflexion of the tradi-tional European tendency to claim a country by simply visiting it.

The rest of the history of Mozambique after its conquest by Portugal follows the same lines as most of the histories of colonial Africa. Soon after the subjugation of the last of the resistance forces the Portuguese proceeded to take possession of our land resources, beginning with those areas which were capable of producing commercial crops such as sisal, cotton, tea, palm-oil, sugar and ground-nuts. These were handed over to large private economic interests which went on to drive the African people off their land. With the help of the Portuguese government they turned most of our people into cheap labour. Wherever there were mineral resources in the country, the Portuguese government appropriated them and sold the right of exploration and exploitation to European economic interests, again turning the traditional African people into cheap labour for the extraction of these resources.

When precious metals such as gold, copper and diamonds were discovered in the neighbouring then colonies of the Rhodesias, the Republic of the Transvaal and the colony of Natal, the Portuguese colonialists seized the opportunity of getting a share out of the business by selling cheap Mozambique African labour to the companies which were engaged in mining. This was the beginning of the now traditional tendency of Mozambicans migrating in large numbers to the neighbouring countries to seek employment. When the Portuguese noticed that more and more Africans were migrating to the Transvaal, the Cape and other industrial areas of southern Africa to work in mining, they arranged to harness the labour force, control it and bargain for more financial gains for themselves. With the Transvaal and now the so-called Republic of South Africa, the Portuguese clinched quite a number of profitable agreements, such as the 1875 treaty between Portugal and the Transvaal Republic which was later revised in 1901, 1928, 1934, 1936, 1940, 1950 and is now under consideration for another revision. The essential point in these agreements is that the economic interests which are now represented by the Transvaal Chamber of Mines are to be granted large-scale labour recruiting privileges in the southern part of Mozambique in return for guarantees that a certain proportion of the sea-borne traffic to the industrial zone of the Transvaal, that is, the Witwatersrand area of Johannesburg and Pretoria, must pass through the port of Lourenço Marques rather than through the rival South African ports of Durban, East London, Port Elizabeth and Capetown. In the latest revision of the agreement the proportion of goods to be shipped from this area through Lourenço Marques is 45·5 per cent.

Other points figuring prominently in this agreement are: (a) direct monetary payments per African recruited, which now amounts to 35 shillings per head; (b) guarantees to repatriate Mozambique workers if found anywhere in South Africa outside of the contract arrangements included in the agreement; (c) a maximum contract time of 18 months, and the permission to establish Portuguese Native Affairs inspection stations within the Republic of South Africa.

In order to make certain that enough African workers will sign up for work in South Africa under this agreement, the Portuguese government passed a series of laws restricting the free choice of employment within Mozambique, aimed specifically at that class of people who are needed in the mining system of South Africa. While the language and tone of these laws might appear to those accustomed with European jurisprudence to be aimed at discouraging vagrancy and laziness, their actual effect is to force individuals who are employed in their own traditional economic enterprises to migrate to South Africa. The latest of these laws states that any African who does not work for a European or Asian or so-called 'civilized' African, or anyone who is not engaged in cash-producing economic activities must be arrested and forced to sign a contract with any of the various economic interests in Mozambique or abroad. These are the notorious 'contract labour laws'. Since in Mozambique itself there are not enough industries to employ most of the able-bodied men of our country, hundreds of thousands of people must sign contracts with South African and Rhodesian mining companies for work in those countries at wages much below subsistence levels. Every year there are over 100,000 Mozambican men who take up employment in the gold mines of the Transvaal and the Orange Free State alone. More than 200,000 other Mozambican workers are also employed in South African plantations, farms, homes and secondary industries. Estimates for Northern and Southern Rhodesia run to 150,000, mostly employed in copper mining, farming and white homes. More than 100,000 northern Mozambicans are forced by the same law to seek employment in Tanganyika, Zanzibar and Kenya, mostly in sisal plantations, railways and harbours and as servants in European and Asian homes and as night watchmen.

We Mozambicans, therefore, have the largest number of people working outside of their national boundaries in the whole continent of Africa. We are persecuted and exploited at home and used as slave labour abroad. Students of modern economic and labour practices have described our situation, and that of our brother Angolans and Guineans (under Portuguese rule) as being that of modern slavery. Modern slavery is defined as a system of labour exploitation in which the slave owner does not take any responsibility for the welfare of the human being he uses. The Portuguese government makes profits out of us, while at the same time the various economic interests which make direct use of us accumulate large profits. Therefore, we can conclude, on the basis of the facts above, that Mozambique is a slave reservoir for both Portugal and the economic interests controlling the major industries of Southern, Central and East Africa.

As you see, I have cited only one phase of Portuguese colonialism, probably the one that typifies Portuguese policies as against those of the British, the French and the Belgians. There are, however, a whole range of colonial practices which Portugal engages in for which the Mozambican citizen suffers tremendously. These include, among others, direct imposition of Portuguese legal, religious, moral and social systems upon our people without even the slightest regards for our feelings. The denial of political rights to the majority of the people of Mozambique is another typical characteristic of Portuguese colonialism. Racial discrimination in all situations where Europeans and Africans live and work in the same area is as typical a Portuguese practice as it is of all colonial powers, despite Portuguese claims to the contrary.

If you add to the above an educational system whereby the children of more than 99 per cent of the population are denied schools, except for a bare ten per cent of them who get some Christian mission schools, while the children of less than 1 per cent of the population enjoys educational facilities up to university, then you have a perfect situation for breeding a society of slaves.

It is against this kind of colonialism that the *Mozambique Liberation Front* arose. The *Mozambique Liberation Front* is a reaction against foreign domination. It is a revolt against European and foreign exploitations. It's a movement against modern slavery. It's a movement organized to fight for the restoration of our political freedom. Through the *Mozambique Liberation Front* we wish to complete the process of regaining the self-respect and dignity of the African person. It is a movement which is determined to take over from where our heroic forebearers left off at the last century and develop our people to new heights of achievement in the economic field, in science, the fine arts and religion. We want to be the free people that we once were, and more. We want to join the rest of the free peoples of Africa to form a United Africa and a United, Free and Peaceful World.

While the beginning of the organization itself is simple and dates from June 1962, the spirit behind the *Mozambique Liberation Front* derives from long years of suffering through exploitation, beatings, tortures, exiling, separation, etc., of our people by the Portuguese colonial government over the last 75 years. It is the result of the action of a new generation of Mozambicans who will not subject themselves to indignities by anyone. The *Mozambique Liberation Front* is the crystallization of the spirit of freedom implanted in us by our ancestors and fanned by the strong wind of change now blowing all over Africa.

Historically, the *Mozambique Liberation Front* came out of the union of a number of Mozambican nationalist movements, specifically the Mozambique African National Union, União Democratica Nacional de Moçambique and União Nacional Moçambicana de Independencia. These groups had started their work independently in various parts of Southern and East Africa. The Mozambique African National Union (MANU) started in Mombasa, prompted by Mozambican members of the Kenya African National Union. Later it combined with political groups organized in Tanganyika, and finally established its headquarters in Dar es Salaam, Tanganyika. While many of its members had been active members of KANU and TANU after the independence of Tanganyika they began to concentrate on organizing their own people against Portuguese colonialism.

The União Democratica Nacional de Moçambique was started in Southern Rhodesia by a group of young Mozambicans who were working mostly in Salisbury. In 1961 when Tanganyika appeared to be clearly moving towards final independence, several of the leaders of the group decided to move on to Dar es Salaam. For a while after arriving in Dar, it appeared as though there might be an immediate union of the two organizations, but unfortunately personal ambitions of some of the individuals in both parties blocked the action. Later on the UNAMI leaders, who were mostly from the Tete area of Mozambique, also moved to Dar es Salaam. So that for a while there existed in Dar es Salaam no less than three political organizations all of whom claimed to represent the people of Mozambique.

During the time previous to the independence of Tanganyika, I was working in the trusteeship department of the United Nations Organization in New York, as a research officer in connexion with information from Tanganyika, South West Africa and the British Cameroons. I often received letters, documents and petitions from various organizations in all Portuguese colonies, pleading that the United Nations take action against Portugal. After correspondence with several of these groups I began to receive personal letters asking me to join this group or that group as one of its leaders. All three of the above Mozambique political organizations wrote to me asking me to join them individually, but I insisted that the only way I can join a political party for the independence of Mozambique is if they would promise to take immediate steps to unite with other Mozambique groups forming a united front. After all of these three groups had promised that they would, I then came to Dar es Salaam and helped to organize the conference in which the Mozambique Liberation Front was formed.

On establishing FRELIMO, however, we decided to do away with all previously existing organizations and concentrate on the development of the new body, for fear that if we kept the parent organizations, we might waste valuable and scarce talent by working at cross purposes instead of pulling together in one party. However, when the former president of UDENAMO failed to get support for his candidacy for the presidency of FRELIMO, he left Tanganyika and from a foreign African country he announced the dissolution of FRELIMO, calling for the formation of a new front. But since he was speaking only for himself and a couple of other disgruntled fellows, he did not get any support. He kept floating from one African country to another arguing that UDENAMO was not within FRELIMO. While I was still finishing my contract as professor at an American university, preparing to return to East Africa to assume my duties as president of FRELIMO, the gentleman who had been elected secretary-general of FRELIMO became involved in a number of quarrels with other members of the organization. On being disciplined for his part in the disturbances which followed, he and a small number of his supporters were asked to leave Tanganyika and from a foreign African country he also revived another UDENAMO party. So that from time to time you may read in the newspapers about the existence of a UDENAMO representative saying this or that against FRELIMO or UDENAMO against UDENAMO.

While we were attending the Addis Ababa conference of the Heads of State for the establishment of the Organization of African Unity one of the two UDENAMO fellows, aided by the head of the bureau of African affairs of one of the African states, gathered together a number of people, most of whom had been disciplined by FRELIMO for various reasons, and each one claiming to represent a different political party, announced the dissolution of FRELIMO and the formation of a new front in Kampala, Uganda. But when the Uganda government investigated the matter and discovered that this was the work of the same fellow who had previously announced the dissolution of FRELIMO from another African capital, they asked him to move out of the country. Finally, last October, again while a number of the top leaders of FRELIMO were away on diplomatic tours abroad, the director of the bureau of African affairs of the same country which had been supporting one of the UDENAMOs, dispatched

157

a member of his staff to Dar es Salaam, who scooped together a number of Mozambican refugees and in the name of his protegée announced for the third time the dissolution of FRELIMO and the formation of the same new front. And for the tird time in one year the stunt came to nothing. So much for the internal squabble.

In the meantime, soon after the formation of the Mozambique Liberation Front, it was decided that there should be a conference that same year which would formulate the main lines of the policy of the new organization and elect a group of officers who would carry out its work. The congress was to meet in Dar es Salaam, and would be attended by delegates representing the various political groups of Mozambique exiled in East Africa, and as many others as could send delegates from within Mozambique.

In the last half of the month of September, the congress finally took place, attended by 80 delegates and more than 500 observers from Dar es Salaam, Tanga, Lindi, Morogoro, Songea, etc., in Tanganyika, where there are more than 100,000 Mozambicans working in various spheres of life, including thousands of refugees who had just recently arrived from Mozambique. There were also observers from Zanzibar, an island off the coast of Tanganyika, where over 30,000 Mozambicans work in shipping and clove farms and plantations; from Mombasa, Kenya came several people representing a Mozambican community of over 200,000 in the dockyards; and a few came from the Rhodesias and Nyasaland. All in all, the first congress of our party was a very representative affair, in spite of the fact that it was the first of its kind in the history of our country.

The congress of FRELIMO examined carefully the present situation in Mozambique and made recommendations for the Central Committee to carry out during the year. During the discussions of the congress, the following points were noted: (a) that the people of Mozambique were still under the subjection of Portuguese colonialism, characterized by political, economic, social and cultural oppression; (b) that the Portuguese government in Mozambique denied the basic freedoms to which modern man is entitled; (c) that the Portuguese government failed to recognize the primacy of the interests of the Mozambicans, and that it opposed the right of the people to determine their own destinies, continuing to insist upon labelling Mozambique as an 'overseas province'; (d) that Portugal, instead of seeking a peaceful solution to the conflict between her and the people of Mozambique, continued to use fascist methods of repression, reinforcing the military and police apparatus by the dispatch of military contingents, massacring innocent people, imprisoning and torturing people suspected of nationalistic tendencies. The congress noted further that as a result of the above facts, the people of Mozambique were being forced to seek effective methods of self-defence. It also considered that the recent reforms promulgated by Portugal were within the framework of the same colonialist spirit that has typified Portuguese action for centuries; that because they were taken unilaterally, even if they were fair to the people, they would still be unacceptable. The congress, therefore, called upon all Mozambican patriots to unite under FRELIMO's banner to fight for the independence of their country. It went on to call attention to the existence of an alliance between the racist powers of Portugal, South Africa and the so-called Central African Federation, led by Salazar, Verwoerd and Welensky, aided by a multifarious system of economic interests financed in London and New York, and urged all freedom-loving peoples of the world to condemn and act in such a way as to frustrate the inhuman activities of these forces.

The congress of FRELIMO declared its determination to promote the efficient organization of the struggle of the Mozambican people for national liberation and adopted the following measures to be carried out by the Central Committee:

(1) Development and consolidation of the organization of FRELIMO;

(2) Development of unity among Mozambicans;

(3) Maximum utilization of the energies and capabilities of each member of FRELIMO;

(4) To promote and accelerate the training of cadres;

(5) To use every effort to expedite the access of Mozambique to freedom;

(6) To promote the social and cultural development of Mozambican women;

(7) To develop literacy programmes for Mozambican people, creating schools wherever possible;

(8) To encourage and support the formation and consolidation of trade unions, student and women's organizations.

(9) To encourage as much as possible, cooperation with nationalist organizations of Angola, Guinea and Cape Verde;

(10) To procure all means of self-defence and prepare the people for every eventuality;

(11) To appeal for financial support from organizations which sympathize with the cause of the people of Mozambique;

159

(12) To establish permanent centres of information and propaganda in all parts of the world;

(13) To seek diplomatic, moral and material help for the cause of freedom in Mozambique, especially from the already independent states of Africa, and from all peaceful and freedom loving countries of the world.

I am sure you would also be interested in knowing about what FRELIMO is doing to implement at least some of these decisions by the congress. As you may realize it would be unwise for me to give you any indication of what we are doing to implement those resolutions which have to do with direct action within Mozambique. There are, however, two areas of action we can freely outline publicly without danger. These are: *diplomatic action* and *education*. Since the formation of FRELIMO, and even before, diplomatic contacts have been intensified in all parts of the world. For example, we have made certain that our point of view is well understood by those committees of the United Nations which are directly responsible for gathering information on Portuguese colonies. Consequently, as soon as the meetings of the congress ended, I flew back to New York to petition the Fourth Committee of the General Assembly when our territory was being discussed. We also intensified our contacts with international conferences in Africa, Asia and the Americas. At the annual conference of PAFMECSA which met at Leopoldville, Congo, Mr Uria Simango, the vice-president of FRELIMO, presented a petition on our behalf. At the Moshi Conference of the Afro-Asian Solidarity Council, we sent a team of five members of the Central Committee who shared the responsibility of presenting our case in the United States, I attended the first Negro Leadership Conference on Africa, where I presented a background paper on conditions in Mozambique and participated in imformal discussions, giving substantive information to the delegates. Our university students in Europe and North America also carry the responsibility of informing their fellow-students on Mozambique whenever they attend international student conferences. They have a student organization, Uniao Nacional dos Estudantes de Moçambique (UNEMO), which works in close cooperation with FRELIMO. We believe that our case against Portuguese colonialism deserves to be known by all people of the world. We also hope that through this knowledge the representatives of the peace loving peoples of the world will be able to take the proper steps to convince Portugal of the stupidity of her position.

Finally, we have launched a crash programme for educational advancement for the people of Mozambique.

I have made reference to the almost complete lack of education for the black peoples of Mozambique. The congress of FRELIMO, taking into account the sad state of educational facilities in our country under Portuguese colonialism, has asked the Central Committee to study the education of the Mozambique people as a priority matter.

In response to this situation, the Central Committee of FRELIMO has divided the problem into three levels of action: the university level, the secondary school level and the mass literacy level. At the university level it was decided that we should send out to all countries any available Mozambicans with educational background equivalent to secondary school. For this purpose we have sent out to most independent countries of the world requests for scholarships for Mozambicans for education in any school above the secondary level. We have also appealed to the United Nations to do all it can to help us in this respect. Consequently, we have received offers for scholarships in many countries in Eastern Europe, North and South America and Western Europe. So far we have been able to send out students to the United States of America, where facilities for both training and transportation were liberally given by governmental and private bodies; to Western Europe, especially France, where training especially in medicine is being given to several Mozambicans, and Italy, in law and economics. We also have some students in the Soviet Union, taking courses in various fields of study, including technology. We have more scholarships offered to us than we can take. Therefore, with a generous grant from a private foundation in the United States, the Mozambique Institute (Instituto Moçambicano) has been formed under the directorship of my wife, Janet, in Dar es Salaam. This Institute is separate from the political body of FRELIMO, but caters to the needs of the refugees from Mozambique who have yet to complete their secondary education. The institute will provide housing for 50 students, and educational and cultural facilities for any Mozambican refugees who wish to partake of them. The Institute's activities also include a general survey of the refugees in Tanganyika and neighbouring countries in order to assess the number and needs of these people. In addition, literacy programmes are needed to reach the millions of our people who are not able to read or write. We believe that without at least literacy, our efforts for a stable, progressive and peaceful Mozambique cannot be crowned with success. We, therefore, appeal to all those who believe in the effectiveness of these programmes to give us whatever help they can afford.

We have already sent out to various parts of the world a number of Mozambican students who are now pursuing their studies in different fields of learning in America, Europe, and Asia.

I shall not discuss here that phase of our programme which is being done within Mozambique for security reasons, except to say that it is proceeding as scheduled. Nor can I with impunity engage in any analysis of our military training programme, which is also going on.

Our diplomatic work has been intensified since our congress. We have opened a number of offices in several African independent states; in Europe, America and Asia we depend mostly upon our students for representation, who constantly distribute information to the various organizations interested in our struggle.

During the months of October, November and December, I, as President of FRELIMO, undertook a long trip to America, Europe and the People's Republic of China, to present Mozambique's case against Portugal. At the United Nations, I petitioned against Portugal and made representations in West Germany against reported economic activities in Portuguese African colonies by some of the big German financial interests. I also stimulated interest in our situation among the West German press, radio and television, calling the German people's attention to those relations between their government and the Salazarist colonial régime which we consider detrimental to our struggle. In West Germany I find a great deal of interest from among the rank and file people. The press, radio and television gave me an ample opportunity to state our case. Educational organizations showed interest in giving us places in their colleges and universities, which we hope to take up soon.

While at the United Nations, I assisted the nine representatives of the Organization of African Unity who were carrying our conversations on the future of Mozambique, Angola and Guinea with Portuguese representatives at the office of the Secretary General, Mr U Thant. My function during these conversations was to expose the veiled attempts by Portugal to hoodwink the African representatives and the people of the world concerning the status of our country. The Portuguese representatives were claiming that the 'organic law for overseas provinces', which the Portuguese parliament rubber-stamped last August, was aimed at applying the principles of self-determination to the colonies of

Portugal in Africa. I called the attention of the delegates to the fact that contrary to what Portugal was saying, this new law was in fact completing the incorporation of our country into Portugal as a province, instead of giving more and more self-government. After reading the law itself, the African statesmen saw the point, and suspended the conversations, insisting that Portugal declare first unequivocally that she is ready to apply the right of self-determination to the people of her colonies in Africa; secondly, that she take immediate steps to discuss with the representatives of Mozambique, Angola and Guinea how she will hand over the economic, political and other instruments for an independent government. In my petition in the Fourth Committee of the United Nations General Assembly, I urged that the member states act on the resolution passed last July by the Security Council. I gave further evidence concerning the support which Portugal receives from several members of the North Atlantic Treaty Organization, including the United States, Great Britain, France and West Germany, almost in that order. I cited the fact that Portugal continues to receive weapons from these powers, even though it has been proved beyond doubt that these weapons are now being used by Portugal against us in Africa. I also called attention to the various arrangements being made by these same NATO powers to prop the Portuguese economy during this period of crisis in her colonies. I demand that the United Nations be called upon to condemn these criminal acts.

During the months of November and December, Brother Marcelino dos Santos, external affairs secretary of FRELIMO, visited the People's Republic of China to initiate conversations which I later completed when I also visited China. Our visit to China was aimed at seeking aid from the people of that country, and to strengthen our position against Portuguese colonialism. While there we thanked the Chinese people for their solidarity with the peoples of Africa in their struggle against colonialism and imperialism.

On his way back from China, Brother dos Santos, joined by Brother Simango, FRELIMO's vice-president, visited several Eastern and Western European countries, including the Soviet Union, Poland, East Germany, Czechoslovakia, Italy and France, in all of which they sought aid of all kinds.

On my way back from China, I stopped in India, and since then I have been making representations to the government of that country to see if they could help us in various ways, including providing educational facilities for some of our Portuguese-speaking students, making use of the vast educational resources and experience of that country.

Summary

As it can be seen from the foregoing, our struggle is a difficult one. Portugal as a colonial power has almost no resemblance to any other modern colonial power. She is a dictatorship; she is backward in every way conceivable; and she has no desire to conform with the principles of self-determination approved by all the international organizations of which she is a member.

Therefore, there is no other means of bringing her to the conference table for the discussion of our independence. Instead, Portugal is taking steps to incorporate further our country by passing new laws to that effect; she is building an ever increasing military force to suppress our people and is putting in prison, torturing, killing and exiling thousands of some of the most courageous of our freedom fighters.

Yet the writing is clear on the wall of Portuguese colonialism: Portugal will scram out of Mozambique! The Mozambique Liberation Front is determined to hasten the day on which our people will be free.

3

Message from the Women of Mozambique
to
The World Congress of Women
14–17 June, 1969

Madame Chairman,
Distinguished Delegates,
Comrades and Friends,
ON behalf of the struggling people of Mozambique and on behalf of the Mozambique Liberation Front (FRELIMO), the vanguard of the fighting people of Mozambique, and on behalf of the women of Mozambique, whom we have the honour of representing, and on behalf of the Council of the Presidency of FRELIMO, we would like to convey our warmest greetings and revolutionary salutes first of all, to this august Conference of the militant and peace-loving women of the world; to the Women's International Democratic Federation; and particularly to the hosts, the Finnish Women's Organization and the People of Finland.

Secondly, we would like to express our happiness and deep appreciation of having been given the opportunity to participate in this historic Conference, for it will enable us to learn and share the experiences traversed by other women of the world in their determined struggle against imperialism, colonialism and other evil forms of exploitation and deprivation of human rights and dignity.

Thirdly, we would like to express our strong wish and hope that the efforts and aims, endeavours and objectives of this important Conference, which is going to discuss thoroughly and exchange viewpoints on the complex problems of the role and fate of the women in the struggle for emancipation of mankind will be crowned with complete success, for we believe that the results of our consolidation could help the remnant part of mankind still under the yoke of colonialism and imperialism in its bitter struggle for complete elimination of these vicious systems of exploitation of man by man, and for the attainment of national independence and freedom.

National independence and freedom are essential for a people who wish to carry out the task of social revolution to achieve the total emancipation of man from the old patterns and trends of life.

Madame Chairman
and
Fellow Delegates,

Our interest in this Conference is, as we said earlier, to learn from, and share the experiences of, other women of the world who fight the powerful enemy of the people's revindication. Perhaps we have not a great contribution to give you except our long and bitter experience of almost five hundred years of subservience, slavery and exploitation. Our experience in organized armed struggle against the fascist colonial domination of Portugal is small; it is of almost five years duration, although important victories have been scored by our people since FRELIMO proclaimed the general armed insurrection against the Portuguese colonialism on 25 September 1964.

If this Conference were meeting ten years ago, many of you might be asking yourselves the question, 'Mozambique! Where is that?' Today Mozambique is a name which is often linked in the press with the words 'Forgotten war', or, 'a blanket of silence' followed by a story which is far from forgettable and which shouts its glad strength and deep sorrows to the world. To understand the Mozambican woman, you must see in your mind our country, for we are inextricably a part of the spirit of the land from which we come and with it we grow side by side.

The statistics of Mozambique are simple; it lies on Africa's south-east coast, covers about 300,000 square miles and has a population of between 7½ and 8 million people. The country is primarily agricultural. The export of human labour to South Africa and Rhodesia is an extremely important part of Mozambican colonial economy. Our people are 98 per cent illiterate; 94 per cent of the population are peasants living at a subsistence level; when they earn a wage in their farming activities it is less than 1/40th of the annual wage of a Portuguese settler. It is a land of beauty, of green hills, cool rivers and golden plains, but it is a land of old men, tired women, and little children.

But the basic fact one must understand about our country is that it is a land suffering under the heavy yoke of Portuguese colonialism, soaked with the brutalities of a fascist colonial police system, its people oppressed in the struggle for food and shelter in the quest for sheer survival.

The story of Mozambique as a colony is a long one, dating back to the end of the fifteenth century when Vasco da Gama landed there in 1498. But the people never accepted colonial rule and rebellions continued until the 1920s. Then, on 16th June, 1960, occurred the massacre at the town of Mueda in northern Mozambique when over 500 Africans were killed, more than eight times the number massacred at the infamous Sharpeville brutality in the Republic of South Africa. But the world heard nothing of the murders of Mueda, for the Portuguese were especially refined in their techniques of blinding the eyes of the world and laying at rest any curious minds which inquired that indeed her colonies were havens of peace and harmony. On the contrary, the seven colonial possessions of Portugal in Africa and Asia are far from states of quietude, and without doubt, those populations will one day find the freedom they seek.

The political system of Mozambique has always been centred in Lisbon from where the Portuguese Governor-General of the colony received his orders and where the laws are made. A network of Portuguese officials carry out the day to day control of the African population and where once traditional African chiefs were sources of authority for our people, they are now appointed by the colonial government and their powers removed. To avoid condemnation as a colonial power at the United Nations, in 195? Portugal passed legislation which made our country a 'Province of Metropolitan Portugal instead of a colony, but the change in name has made no difference in the system of administration.

Hand in hand with the political administration are the commercial companies which have extraordinary powers over the African people that live in the areas given to them by Portugal to exploit. For instance, in areas controlled by cotton-producing companies where the population is forced to grow that crop, the average annual income is £5, and then ⅛th of the income must be paid out in taxes! This concession system, the economic system which the colonial régime has used to gain riches from the land, has caused untold hardships in our lives, and driven our husbands and sons to seek work in neighbouring countries. In reality, what has happened as a result of the colonial economic system is the emergence of an apartheid régime not unlike that of South Africa. The Portuguese claim to have 'civilized' about 4½ thousand Africans, but even this so-called assimilated person is discriminated against in every hour of his day – even if he is 'civilized' he is effectively excluded from hotels and restaurants, must carry his identity card, and so on. As for the African person who has not had the opportunity to be 'civilized', freedom of movement is limited, and in the urban areas he must stay in his locations after dark. Educational apartheid is also a part of our lives – it is no wonder when, for example, in 1962, only 4 per cent of the total budget for Mozambique was allocated for education, and that pittance rarely made a contribution to the mind of the black child.

This cruel domination has naturally adversely affected the life of the Mozambican woman. To be brutally frank, she is often more despised than a barnyard animal and is only considered useful as a producer of children, to stay at home where she is the slave of her husband. Since our peasant economy is at a subsistence level, much of the labour of the fields is her responsibility – to first clear the bush, and then to tend the crop under the burning sun or heavy rain, sometimes with hunger in her body. In the end, the fruits of her labour must often go at a low price to the Portuguese concession company which holds the rights over the land. If her husband works at home, the wage he earns is often too little to keep food in the house. But when her husband goes to the mines of South Africa or Rhodesia, she must also find the money to pay the taxes. Too often the tax is heavier than can be paid, and this woman, wife and mother, is arrested and sent to 'xibalo' (forced labour) until she has worked out the payment of the tax for her husband. When the husband is arrested for forced labour, either on the company plantation or sent to the mines, they may be separated for years. It is a common sight to see women walking along the roads, selling wood, food, or some small produce, to support the children. And sometimes she has no alternative but to sell her own body as well. The Portuguese 'colon' sees the African woman as a instrument to satisfy his own personal interest. Prostitution has been encouraged and legalized. A woman is issued an official document to legitimize her status of prostitution. Women do not seek this status, but the empty stomach of one's family can be the mother of desperation.

In the field of education, the tremendous sacrifices of a family to send a child to school is often expended on the male children, so that only a handful of the women in our country can read and write – and remember, the total literacy rate of our people is only 2 per cent! These attitudes towards the women in our society and the deprivation of education for our girls has been a major weapon in the hands of the Portuguese colonial government, for when the women are ignorant and powerless, the nation is weak.

There are very few people in this world who actually enjoy war when they must live in the midst of its horror and hardship. But sometimes there is no alternative, even for people who would much prefer to spend their lives in peace. For us, the government of Portugal left no door through which we could walk to freedom in peace. It was with determination to win our struggle for liberation that our armed forces launched the war in 1964, and that strong spirit has never failed to carry us onward. The Portuguese were taken by surprise and within the first few months they lost control of parts of the northern Provinces. At that time the Portuguese Government tried to make the world believe that it was only a small problem with rebel raiders across the border from Tanzania, but in reality the freedom army was already inside the country. In 1964 we began with only 250 trained guerilla fighters; now we have 10,000 freedom fighters trained and well-equipped in the field, and a militia over the country-side – men, women and children – whose role in the liberation struggle is crucial. Portuguese troops in Mozambique number 60,000 well-armed soldiers; the fascist régime in Lisbon spends almost 50 per cent of its national budget on 'defence'. This past year the casualty rate among enemy troops averages 100 per month, and that rate is this year monthly increasing. In our liberated areas the Portuguese do not dare to venture far from their isolated bases. Last year FRELIMO opened a new offensive in the Tete Province where the infamous Cabora Bassa dam is to be built – a colossal work projected to be the largest dam in Africa. We are determined that the dam will never be built, for not only is it supposed to be a settlement area for one million Portuguese immigrants, but it is to provide electrical power for the Republic of South Africa, a miserable country where the African people continue to endure the terrible hardships imposed by a racist white minority government.

When FRELIMO was formed, the leaders were immediately preoccupied with the mobilization and organization of the people. the Mozambican women played an active role in the clandestine organization in all regions of the country. Before the armed stuggle began, many women had left the country with thier husbands, their children, brothers and friends in order to join FRELIMO to fight for national independence. We were the women of Mozambique with a new role to play, one which won our total devotion and demanded the entire strength of our minds, our bodies and our spirit. We women are a part of this struggle, standing beside our men, ready to give our lives to the heavy tasks that lie before us.

What are those tasks?

In time of war, the political and revolutionary level of the people must be high enough to overcome the many obstacles which they face – the spirit of sacrifices is the spirit of our struggle. It is this mobilization and politication of the people which is her first duty. The masses must gain knowledge of the reality of the struggle, to know FRELIMO, its objectives in the struggle for liberation, to know why we are fighting, against whom we are fighting, and the perspectives for a free Mozambique.

She faces another important task; that is to produce food not only for her family but for our guerrilla fighters as well. Yet it is not only to produce the food. She must often carry food and heavy caskets of ammunition over great distances and difficult countryside, walking for many days or even weeks, sometimes encountering ambushes of the enemy. Her body is as strong as her spirit.

Third, she cares for the special victims of war: our hearts hold close those children who are orphans or who have been separated from their parents – the lost children. They are growing up in our orphanage in the liberated area. Even with little food, few medicines and scarce clothing, we live with them during the war while preparing their lives for the day of peace.

She participates in the health services in first aid units and must comfort the families of victims the war has claimed.

She carries her weapons, and when necessary fights in combat units.

Since the beginning of the armed struggle, our families have

169

had to flee their villages and settle in sheltered areas where the bombs of the Portuguese cannot find us. Now, refugees are returning to Free Mozambique to start life anew. While the war continues on the front lines, we women must build our villages for peace. But we never forget that the oppression of the Mozambican woman was excessive, and for us to be able to reach our objectives it is necessary to exert untiring effort to win our dreams.

These are our tasks. We know we are not alone, for the progressive women of the world will share the burdens we carry.

As a result of our victories on the war front, we are faced with problems which are not different from those of any developing country. We are beginning to build a new society – economically, politically, socially – for the one million people who are already our responsibility. We have established schools where once a child never had the opportunity to even see a book, medical posts and hospitals in which our people are treated for diseases that have plagued them for centuries, organized cottage industries and agricultural cooperatives which have already produced a surplus for export. Forced labour and forced cultivation have ended in the liberated areas, and more than 80 per cent of the land is being farmed for the first time, this time for the benefit of the people, and not for concessionary companies. The task is tremendous and full of difficulties, principally because (1) our cadres for development work are few, for the Portuguese refused to educate and never trained our people for anything but menial labour; and (2) the material aid necessary – tools, educational materials, transport equipment, etc. – can come only from friendly governments and some humanitarian organizations who sympathize with our struggle for national liberation. This means that though our tasks are those of any government struggling to give its people the basic tools to build a stronger social and economic life, the international channels of aid to independent nations are not yet available to us. On the other side, we face the formidable allies of Portugal in her EFTA and NATO alliances. Foreign capital is crucial to the maintenance of that backward and fascist régime, and without that aid the cost of maintaining the army overseas would be prohibitive. We are too often the victims of the mutual fears of European nations. But we shall succeed. We have fought hard for what we have so far won, and we shall somehow build the nation which has been our great hope for our future.

Madame Chairman and Comrades,

The time has come when the Mozambican woman is no longer isolated from the international stage, for the world is on the side of those who fight for a just cause. We are engaged in a life and death struggle and as often as we are given the opportunity to do so, the people of the world will hear our cries of denunciation of colonialism and imperialism especially that of the Portuguese fascist régimes and her allies. We solidly stand with the courageous people of Vietnam from whom we have learned the bitter-sweet lesson of constancy in the face of seemingly endless brutality. We are encouraged by and have joined the ranks of the long-suffering peoples of the world who are fighting bravely to crush the vicious forces of exploitation and oppression which encircle us with the barbed wire of their economic monopolies and fearful weapons of war. The time has come for the people of the world, and for the organizations represented by the women here, the African continent is still not free from colonialism and neo-colonialism. Imperialist powers still quarrel over her riches; millions of people are still held in the grip of colonial rule or minority white fascist domination. We are the people of Mozambique, Angola, Guinea-Bissau, South Africa, Zimbabwe and Namibia. We have for centuries been silenced in our demands for what belongs to us. We are no longer silent, and it is time for the world to listen.

Madame Chairman and Friends,

It is an honour for us to sit here with you in these deliberations. This Congress has heard us and we are glad. The question remains: what can the women of this Congress do to help us in our tasks?

Little more than one week ago my comrades of the Mozambique Delegation and myself were living with the orphans and lost children of the war. The women's section of FRELIMO developed an orphanage in Free Mozambique. We are making an appeal to your women's organizations to help us continue this work, to cooperate with us in sending us material aid for these children, such as special milk, clothing, medicine, and so on. This aid is essential, without it, it is difficult to carry on that part of our work in the liberation struggle. We also ask you to send us simple tools for production – hoes, matchets, axes, sickles, sewing machines, cloth, etc. – and school materials – pencils, erasers, notebooks, slates, and so on.

There are still many things that we could say, but the time is not sufficient to enable us to present a total picture, the truth we know. We, the Mozambican women, would like in this momnet to thank the Presidium of the World Congress of Women as well as the members of the WIDF for the attention paid to our intervention. We hope that, with the contributions yet to come in different commissions of this Congress, the WIDF will be able to carry on more actively its work and will put into practice the resolutions they will adopt.

LONG LIVE THE PEOPLE WHO STRUGGLE FOR NATIONAL LIBERATION!
LONG LIVE THE UNITY OF WOMEN OF THE WORLD!
INDEPENDENCE OR DEATH, WE SHALL WIN!
THE STRUGGLE CONTINUES!

The Women's section of the
Mozambique Liberation Front
(FRELIMO)
16 June 1969
Helsinki, Finland.

Reference Notes

Note

1 Mondlane: *The Struggle for Mozambique*, Penguin African Library, 1969, p. 29.
2 Mondlane; *The Development of Nationalism in Mozambique*, Appendix One, p. 148.
3 The same, p. 139.
4 The same, p. 144.
5 Mondlane: *The Struggle for Mozambique*, p. 119
6 Mondlane: *The Crystallization of a Struggle for Freedom*, Appendix Two, p. 158.
7 Mondlane: *The Struggle for Mozambique*, p. 122.
8 Mondlane: *The Crystallization of a Struggle for Freedom*, Appendix Two, p. 159.
9 Mondlane: *The Development of Nationalism in Mozambique*, Appendix One, p. 149.
10 Mao Tse Tung: *People's Democratic Dictatorship*, Vol. IV, p. 422.
11 Mondlane: *The Struggle for Mozambique*, p. 115.
12 The same, p. 116.
13 The same.
14 Frelimo Documents, Second Congress, Niassa, July 1968.
15 The same.
16 Mondlane: *The Struggle for Mozambique*, p. 126.
17 Giap: *People's War and People's Army*, p. 124.
18 Mondlane: *The Struggle for Mozambique*, p. 128.
19 Mondlane: *The Crystallization of a Struggle for Freedom*, Appendix Two, p. 159.
20 Mondlane: *The Struggle for Mozambique*, p. 130.
21 Frelimo Documents.
22 The same.
23 Mao Tse Tung: *On Tactics Against Japanese Imperialism*, Vol. I, p. 84. Selected Works.
24 Giap: *People's War, People's Army*, p. 84.
25 The same.
26 Mao Tse Tung: *United Front and Independence*, Vol. II, Selected Works.
27 Mondlane: *The Struggle for Mozambique*, p. 150.
28 Frelimo Documents.
29 Giap: *People's War, People's Army*, p. 100.
30 The same, p. 104.
31 Mondlane: *The Struggle for Mozambique*, p. 153/4.
32 The same, p. 146.
33 The same.

34 *Mondlane: Frelimo White Paper*: African Historical Studies, Vol. II p. 332.

35 Mao Tse Tung: *Recruit Large Numbers of Intellectuals*, Vol. II, Selected Works.

36 Mondlane: *The Struggle for Mozambique*, p. 165.

37 The same, p. 147.

38 The same, p. 191.

39 *Mozambique Revolution*, Official Publication of Frelimo, No. 44 June/Sept. 1970. But since then, the Zambesi has been crossed, and fighting has broken out south of the river.

40 Janet Mondlane: *The Role of Women*, Appendix Three, p. 167.

41 The same.

42 Mondlane: *The Struggle for Mozambique*, p. 147.

43 The same, p. 186.

44 The same.

45 The same, p. 112.

46 Frelimo Documents.

47 *Mozambique Revolution*, Vol. 37/38 Jan./April 1969.

48 Mondlane: *The Struggle for Mozambique*, p. 188.

49 The same, p. 189/90.

50 The same, p. 190.

51 The same, p. 191.

52 Frelimo Documents, Second Congress, p. 17.

53 *Mozambique Revolution*, No. 37 Jan./Feb. 1969.

54 Frelimo Documents.

55 Mondlane: *The Struggle for Mozambique*, p. 220/221.

56 The same, p. 222.

57 Kwame Nkrumah: *Class Struggle in Africa*, Panaf Books, 1970, p. 10.

58 The same.

59 Mondlane: *The Struggle for Mozambique*, p. 221/222.

60 Shanti Sadiq Ali on Mondlane: Hindustan Times 8/2/69.

61 *Mozambique Revolution*, Vol. 43 April 1970.

62 The same.

63 Mondlane: *The Struggle for Mozambique*, p. 134.

64 The same, p. 117.

65 *Mozambique Revolution*, No. 43, April 1970.

66 The same.

67 The same.

68 *The Role of the Individual in History*, Plekhanov.

69 *Fundamentals of Marxism*, Lawrence and Wishart, 1969, p. 176.

KWAME NKRUMAH

CLASS STRUGGLE IN AFRICA

HANDBOOK OF REVOLUTIONARY WARFARE

AFRICA MUST UNITE

CONSCIENCISM: NEO-COLONIALISM

DARK DAYS IN GHANA

AXIOMS OF KWAME NKRUMAH (Freedom Fighters'
Edition)

NEO-COLONIALISM, THE LAST STAGE OF
IMPERIALISM

CHALLENGE OF THE CONGO

GHANA, The Autobiography of Kwame Nkrumah

VOICE FROM CONAKRY

CONSCIENCISM: PHILOSOPHY OF DECOLONISATION

Éditions in the West:

THE SPECTRE OF BLACK POWER

THE BIG LIE

RHODESIA FILE MAY OUR

TWO MYTHS

THE PARTICLE DOCTRINES

New material and revisions in this Panaf publication ©
Panaf Kwame Nkrumah

Panaf Books Limited
89 Fleet Street, London, EC4Y 1DR